The Unseen Hand

The experience of a WWII P.O.W. and the Death March of 1945

By Bealer W. Moore

Copyright 2020 by Bealer W. Moore
© the Estate of Bealer W. Moore
All rights reserved.

Library of Congress Cataloging-in-Publication data is available.

ISBN: 978-1-7354482-1-3
Paperback edition

Edited by S. T. Atchison, PhD

MoodSwinger's Press
High Point, NC

Book Design and Cover Design by S. T. Atchison, PhD

Note from the Editor

In the falling light of a September afternoon in 1988, I suffered an emotional hardship. Paw Paw (Bealer) kindly towered over me, grabbed my shoulder and said, "Toddman, this too shall pass." It's a Biblical adage that I've framed as a life mantra, and you're about to see, dear reader, how Paw Paw embodied his advice.

What you hold here is an act of love, so please forgive misspellings of names—personal, place, or otherwise. I worked through two of Paw Paw's transcripts: one handwritten and the other typed. Memoir writing is memory writing—a stream of consciousness—therefore, I moved some portions of the memoir to align with other sections of narrative. At times, the text demonstrates this via italics. I've also added a few footnotes when I discovered pertinent information during research. I also scanned his sketches from the Red Cross sketchbook that he received while in Stalag Luft IV. You'll see these throughout the memoir where the illustration fits the narrative. The rest are found in an Appendix.

I want to thank my wife, Michelle, for helping me "get out of my head," and maintain objectivity when needed.
I want to thank my father-in-law, Glenn H. Horn for his guidance on military jargon, spellings, capitalizations, etc.
I want to thank my uncle, Mark Moore, for his support through this process.
And finally, to my mom, Bealer Gwen Moore, for catching the commas, and helping this memoir get off the ground.

Here's to Paw Paw's legacy,
S. T. Atchison
July, 2020

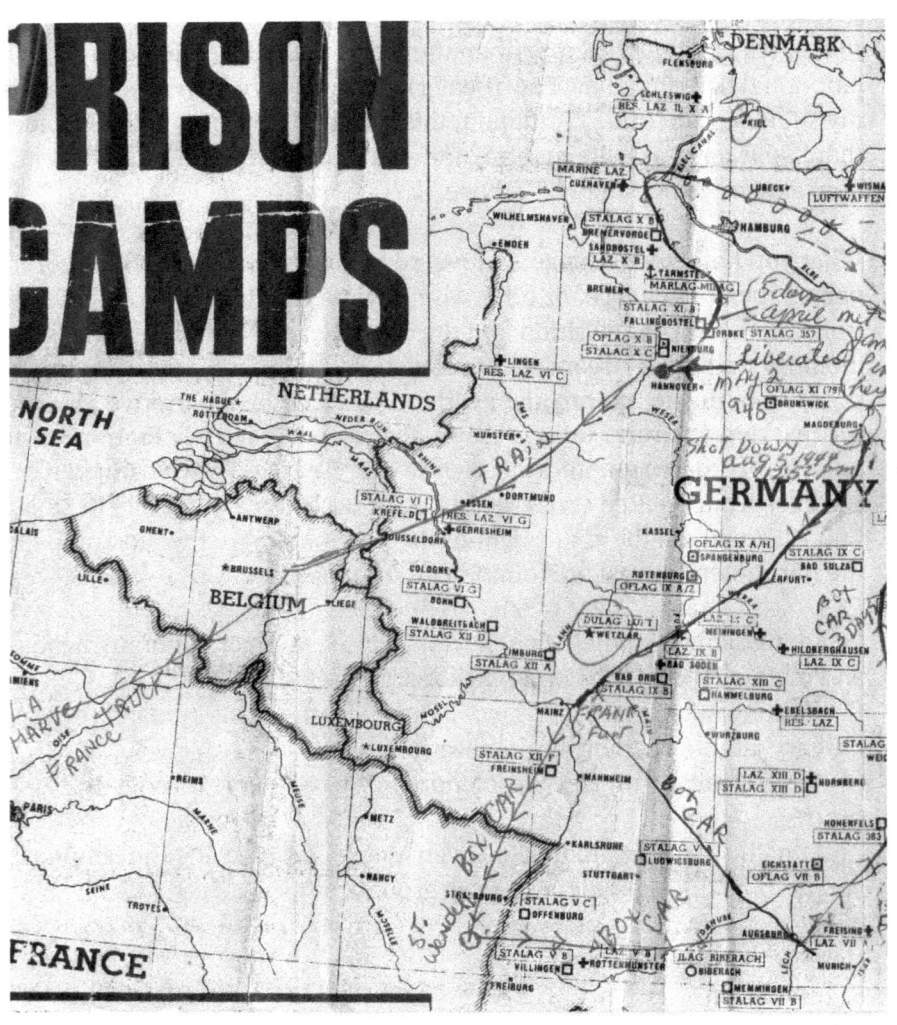

Bealer Moore's route while he was a P.O.W.

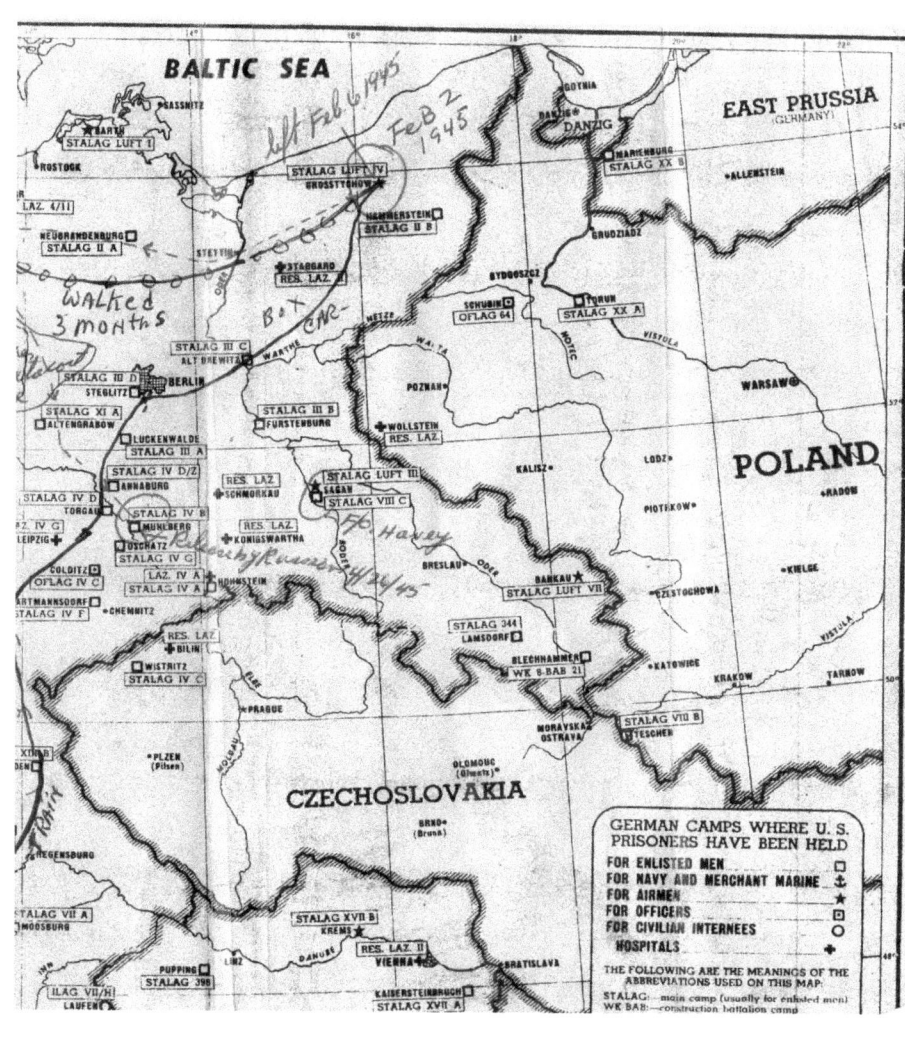

for Nell

"The Unseen Hand"

There's an unknown path before me,
and yet I fear it not.
I know that through all the years gone by,
whatever has been my lot;

that a kind and heavenly father
planned out the way for me.
And I know that in the future
watched over I shall be.

So then, welcome unknown future,
bring me whatever you will.
With God's loving hand to guide me,
I shall be cared for still.

> In His love,
> Brother Royce

Note from the Editor	5
Acknowledgement	11
Chapter 1: Pearl Harbor	17
Chapter 2: Uncle Sam Calls	19
Chapter 3: Training	21
Chapter 4: The Long Flight	29
Chapter 5: Diary of Combat	37
Chapter 6: Premonition	60
Chapter 7: Kaput	67
Chapter 8: The Unseen Hand	72
Chapter 9: Face to Face with the Enemy	77
Chapter 10: Interrogation	87
Chapter 11: Sankt Wendel	95
Chapter 12: Stalag Luft IV	101
Chapter 13: Christmas Eve	113
Chapter 14: Red Cross Telegram	119
Chapter 15: Death March	125
Chapter 16: Experiences on the March	130
Chapter 17: Liberation	149
Afterword	158
Appendix A: Red Cross Sketchbook	161
Appendix B: Copy of Letter	207
Appendix C: Testimony of Dr. Caplan	209
About the Author	222

Acknowledgement

I dedicate this book to my wife Nell who has been by my side for 56 golden years and has shared my love, heartaches, disappointments, joys, and sometimes madness without very little complaints, just accepting me and my faults, which are many.

She can't understand why I don't worry about too much in life. I believe in the song that I sing a lot at nursing homes, "One Day at a Time." This is the way that I try to live my life. Nell has never encouraged me to write a book about my experiences during World War Two. I have often heard her say to others that she would like to forget the war years: receiving the Red Cross telegram stating that I was missing in action, then the telegram stating that I was a prisoner of war, and to add another great burden, she was pregnant at this time with our first child, Bealer Gwen.

Men and women who went through the war often forget or don't give much credit to the ones that they left behind who had also faced some very difficult times. Probably the worst times were those spent worrying about their loved ones in combat, not knowing if they would come home, and if they did, what condition they would return home in. While in the service most don't think about the conditions at home, or worry much about them, except if one is expecting a child, or if one has a mother or father that is approaching old age or might be sick. Some left the farm with aged parents to handle the work and this made it difficult for the ones left behind to carry on the work of farming.

I have often wondered why the Army wanted young men and women. At the average age of high school, young boys are gung-ho and care very little about what is going on in the world around them.

I graduated high school with my girlfriend Nell. All through high school, we were in love. On graduation day on the football field I will never forget what our graduation speaker said that day to our graduating class of 1941. He made the statement that this class will face a terrible time in history, and he could not offer anything encouraging to our class. He certainly knew what he was talking about.

I have often been asked why I don't write a book about the experiences I went through while a P.O.W. I never gave it much thought until recently. Another reason for not writing about my life in the service or my experiences as a P.O.W. is that I have often wondered when talking to someone about what I went through, I would wonder to myself if they really believed in what I was telling them: that men could be so cruel, so hateful. Many people today still don't believe that the Germans had death camps—camps where they burned their victims, Jews and others by the thousands. They just can't believe that men could be so cruel as to cremate people or shoot them for no reason. Some just can't believe the cruel treatment, or the terrible conditions of people that were forced to work as slaves... they cannot believe when you tell them about seeing a B-17 explode in mid air, sending ten crew members to their deaths—your buddies that you flew with. Words cannot describe combat. You just can't find the words to describe how horrible war really is.

After the war when most of my friends that I grew up with would get together, all had served in either the Marines, Navy, Army, or Air Corps, the conversation would always be about our experiences in the service. After a few years, we all scattered to different parts of the country. Some, I have never seen again. Some have departed this earth. And now, I seldom talk to anyone about the war.

I also dedicate this book to my brother-in-law, Marvin King, who gave me the encouragement to write this book. Marvin lives at Elon College, NC. He is a graduate of Elon College and is now retired. Marvin served in Korea.

I volunteered to help Marvin build a barn in appreciation for his many years of kindness and work to my mother who is ninety-seven years old and lives in Elon. Marvin and I worked on this barn for about one month and during those working hours our conversation would be on religion, politics, and army experiences. Marvin was a good listener. This was the first time I had the opportunity to talk to him about the war and my experiences as a P.O.W. I enjoyed the time together, and the work, and hated to see it end.

He encouraged me to write this book.

I started keeping a diary while in Newfoundland, on my way overseas, about my life in the E.T.O. (European Theater of Operations). All the combat missions are listed in the diary except the last one on August fifth, nineteen hundred and forty-four when I was shot down. I didn't make it back to complete the diary. While in Stalag Luft Four, I was lucky in a drawing to win a book and a pencil. I managed to carry this book hidden in the lining of my overcoat while on the forced march across Germany. I had planned to write about the route and the towns along the way but quickly found out that this was impossible. I was so tired and cold at the end of the march each day that I couldn't write. After the diary, the rest of this book is from my memory of the many terrible but sometimes funny experiences. Not everyday was horrible. When you have a group of approximately twenty-year-old men together every day, something is always going on to either make you laugh or make you cry. We had both. I am sure that I will leave out many experiences that I have forgotten, probably for the best. Yet some I will never forget and will remember for the rest of my days and pray that I will never face again.

I quickly found out the only way to survive and keep from going crazy was to not linger on what was happening to me or not to think 'Why me Lord? What have I done to deserve this?' To think before acting, not to take any chances, to play it safe. I made one terrible mistake, one that I paid for dearly and not only myself but also several other men were also affected by my stupid mistake. No bodily harm or repercussions happened to me or those other men from this act of mine, but I have never forgotten that day. I shall explain later...

The Unseen Hand

"In Memory of Bert Scott and Lloyd Maltibe" B.W. Moore 11.24.44

Chapter 1: Pearl Harbor

I saw my father cross the sky. He hitched a barnstorm with a pilot out of Keysville, Virginia, for a small fee, of course. I was six years old, out in the yard at the time playing with a toy plane that had wooden propellers nailed to a post. We couldn't afford store-bought toys. I buzzed about the yard as the wind made those propellers spin.

My dad loved to fly. On this particular day, he came in so low over our house that I could see the whites of his eyes, beaming with the happiness of angels. His mouth was wide open from laughing so hard; his arm dangled his straw-hat over the side; then, he let the hat go. We ran through the fields to find it. There was hardly a scratch on the hat, just a few broken notches on the rim.

I never forgot seeing that plane. Airplanes have always excited me from a very early age.

When I was in high school, I had a dream. Most dreams just fade away, but this one stayed with me and came true in a few years: I dreamed that I was flying the northern route to England and was dressed in heavy flying clothes because we were flying over frozen tundra.

After graduation from high school I went to Baltimore, Maryland, and went to work in the Glenn L. Martin airplane plant. Working on planes put the icing on the cake. I really enjoyed working at this plant; it was exciting being around all those planes and something new everyday.

One quiet Sunday evening, I was listening to the radio when the news came out about Pearl Harbor. I knew then that my days at Glenn L. Martin would soon be over. I was just the right age for Uncle Sam to call.

Nell, my girlfriend, was still at home with her parents, and I would often go home to see her. We decided in August to get married, because we knew that her mother would never allow her to visit me at an Army base. So, we married on August 27, 1942. We came back to Baltimore for a short two months.

Chapter 2: Uncle Sam Calls

Uncle Sam called in December and a new life was beginning for Nell and me. I decided that I would volunteer because I didn't like the idea of being drafted and would probably wind up in the Infantry, so the only course I had was to enlist. Four of my friends and I went to Danville, Virginia, and joined up. Out of the four, I was the only one selected for the Air Corps. Out of the lot of us, only one was killed in combat. Francis Moore Jackson, a paratrooper, was killed in France. Henry Yarborough told me after the war that he had found the Lord in a foxhole. He became a Baptist minister.

We were all sent to Fort Lee, Virginia. Saying goodbye was a terrible experience for me. It was the only time in my life that

Pvt. Bealer Moore, Miami, FL 12.22.42

I saw my father cry when I said goodbye. He was a veteran of World War One, and probably had an idea of what I might be facing.

I was sent to Miami Beach for basic training. We stayed in a beautiful hotel right on the beach with civilians in one hotel and the Air Corps in the other. It was like this all the way down Miami Beach. We had a white glove inspection every morning. We would fall out on the street every morning for roll-call. It was strange not to see any fences or guards at this base. The food was exceptional, and the hotel dining room was magnificent. Each of the columns in the dining hall had goldfish in the middle. I had never before seen such a dining room.

My stay was very short. I wanted to fly, and they needed Airmen overseas, so my basic training was over. I never carried a rifle or shot one, never had a day of training, never had to learn the Manual of Arms, never a day of K.P. duty (kitchen patrol).

Chapter 3: Training

The first of January 1943, I was on my way to Radio School at Truax Field, Wisconsin. We arrived in Wisconsin in a snowstorm. We had our summer uniform on and nearly froze until we found our winter gear in the boxcar; we couldn't get them on fast enough. Madison, Wisconsin was a silvery, scenic place, almost surrounded by water that was frozen over at this time. Cars would travel over the ice and every weekend men would go out on the ice to fish. They had small shacks on the ice in which they stayed the entire time. They must have enjoyed this but to me it seemed crazy, because of the snow and cold wind on that lake.

Nell came to stay with me at this base and we had a swell time every weekend. The training lasted three months, then off to Kingman, Arizona, for gunnery training. Nell couldn't come to this base; no one received a pass.

Kingman was just a wide place in the road at this time; very near Death Valley, California. The food was decent but you had to take a towel to the mess hall and dust off the metal plates because they had so much dust on

Cpl. Burroughs, Nell, and Bealer in Madison, WI.

them, you couldn't eat unless you cleaned them off. It was so hot that you couldn't touch any metal during the day. Okay, it was terribly hot; sometimes reaching 110 degrees, but at night, one had to wear a jacket and sleep under a blanket. Early in the morning and in the late afternoon was the only time that you had duty.

The training was phenomenal. We trained in a Harvard AT-6 airplane. The pilot would fly the plane, and we would sit in the rear with a 30-caliber machine gun and fire at a target being pulled by another plane. The bullets were freshly painted so that we could tell if we were hitting the target. I enjoyed this training because I liked flying and shooting. The pilot would fly in real close to the target and I would empty my gun; then, he would bank off and go down into the Grand Canyon for a sight seeing trip. It was surreal flying down into that canyon.

I was glad to graduate from this place. There really wasn't much for us to do except get into some kind of trouble on occasion.

At this base we had a chickenshit corporal that made us pick up cigarette butts when we were not in training. We never had a pass at this base, and it was sometimes hard to find anything to do but just lie around and talk, no swimming pool, they were digging one by hand and sometimes they would make us dig for the exercise.

When we were flying, we would fly over a ranch house about five miles from the field, nothing but sagebrush between the ranch house and the airstrip. One Sunday, two buddies and I decided that we would hike over to this house; we knew someone was living there so we filled up our canteens and headed out across the runway then into the sage brush which was about one foot high. When we reached the cabin, we saw an old rancher sitting on the front porch in a

The Unseen Hand

rocking chair. When we came up to the porch, we introduced ourselves and told him we often flew over his house. He then asked us what part of the country we came from. We told him and he then said, "I knew you were damn fools not from this part of the country. I have been watching you all the way across that field and kept looking to see when one of you would be hit!"

We asked him what he meant by getting hit.

He said, "No one but a damn fool would cross over that many rattlesnakes, between my house and that runway. Come on, follow me." We followed him around the house. "I want to show you something."

He had dug a well that was about ten feet deep with a four by four across the top and a rope tied in the middle to help him out of the well. "Look under the bush" And there we saw a dead rattler about four feet long.

He said, "I was digging on

"We met that rattler over the ridge behind us."

Saturday and my wife called me to lunch. I happened to look up and saw the rattler lying across the four by four. I hollered for my wife and she shot the rattler. So, on your way back, it's best if you all would use the road."

Using the road was the long way around, but he didn't have to ask us again. That air base had more rattlers than men.

We shot clay pigeons everyday and I really got a kick out of shooting that shotgun. For the first time in my life I got to shoot a shotgun as much as I wanted to. At the base we had a shooting range, a track, and we would fire at targets that were thrown out of the trap house. Some "birds" were released low to the ground; others were in a trap house about ten feet high. We had orders that if a low house didn't fire a clay target, to go and find out why they didn't shoot. These trap houses were on the ground, so many times a rattler would crawl into the shade of these houses; the man inside would not throw his clay to let us know that a rattlesnake was close by. We would then go and kill the snake. This happened almost every day. We had turns in the low house throwing the targets, and we kept a close eye on the open back of that house.

After graduation from gunnery school, I was sent to Salt Lake City where I was to meet with our crew, but the headlines on the paper caused me to think about what I was heading for. It read: Ninety Planes Missing Over Germany. It was just too damn hot over there for me at this time, so I joined the Air Corps Cadets. I was sent to Texas A. & M. College to start cadet training.

Training as an Aviation Cadet was quite an experience and there were only two things that I liked about it: Nell was with me, and I was learning to fly. The food here was outstanding, but the subjects in college were hard. I failed Calculus with about half of my class. This course made me realize that I was not college material–although I passed the other subjects.

One thing that I hated about this part of my training was the chickenshit upperclassmen. They gave me a lot of trouble and seemed to know every time that I would not obey the rules. I had to walk gigs every Sunday, but Nell would be there with me watching me walk for about three hours.

The only good thing about the training was they needed someone that could blow a bugle and they found out on my service record that I could blow one. I knew all the calls; so, they made me the bugler. I had a pass to come and go anytime I wanted to. I could leave the college and walk down to Nell's room about one mile away; this I enjoyed. I would blow Taps about ten o'clock, but I had to be up early to blow Reveille at six o'clock. The other cadets were not allowed many privileges, and couldn't go anywhere alone. They were always in a group.

Bealer playing bugle, 1943

After training here, I was sent down to San Antonio, Texas, for one of the hardest tests that I have ever taken; it lasted four hours. I failed. That ended my Cadet training, and my chances of being a pilot.

I honestly never regretted that I washed-out as a Cadet.

I was ready for overseas duty. I was sent to Tampa, Florida, to join my crew. We stayed there for two days. Then someone did a stupid thing: they gave us a ten-day delay in route to go ninety miles to Avon Park, Florida. So I went home. I did another foolish thing: I stayed four days longer at home and was A.W.O.L.(absent without leave)–the only time in the service, and I paid for this mistake.

My fine was thirty dollars, busted down to Pvt, and restricted to the base for one week. Nell was with me at this time; this was the part of the penalty I didn't like. The rest of the crew would cover for me when they would come around and check in on me by telling them that I had gone to the P.X. (post exchange) or the U.S.O. Club (United Service Organizations). I never got caught.

I had not met my pilot before this nor any of the other officers on the crew. Lt. Bert Scott, the pilot, knew that I was a washed-out cadet, and he knew I was four days A.W.O.L. He also knew that most washed-out cadets were misfits.

Some of these cadets were very bitter. Some had a reason to be bitter because they were sent to the infantry. One thing the pilot didn't know about me was the fact that I wasn't bitter. I was glad to be out of that chickenshit outfit. Meeting him for the first time, with four days A.W.O.L., he must have thought he had one screwball of a radio operator. He found out later that I could do my job and was never slack in doing what was required of me. We became good friends, and he knew that I was on the ball while flying. That Joker was the one Yankee out of the seven that I liked. Only three of us out of the ten were Southerners.

We trained at Avon Park for three months, practicing bomb runs down to Cuba, and night flights up to Greenville, South Carolina. It was on a night flight to Greenville that our pilot lost his cool. (The other time was over Germany on a mission...)

We made the flight to Greenville okay, but on the return trip to Avon Park, the pilot called the navigator for a heading, and the navigator was listening to music on the radio, and he had no idea where we were. We were lost and found ourselves over water. We didn't know if it was the Gulf of Mexico or the Atlantic Ocean. The pilot called me to send out an S.O.S. for a radio heading. We finally got a homing signal from Tampa, and we ran out of gas landing at that base.

We never heard music on the plane after that.

I enjoyed our stay and our training at Avon Park, but all good things must come to an end. Our training was over, and we were ready for our duty in combat.

Nell and Bealer Moore - 1943

Chapter 4: The Long Flight

When our training was over at Avon Park, we received our orders to head overseas. We didn't know where we were going, but thought it might be England.

We were praying it would be England.

Saying goodbye to Nell, who was pregnant at this time, was the hardest thing I had ever faced before. We stayed in Avon Park with an old couple who treated us like we were their children. We would play a card game called Rook with them at night, and he would take me fishing on my days off.

The morning I left, he and his wife were crying with us. In talking with Nell many times about what I would face overseas, I always believed that I would not complete my missions, but I also believed that I would not be killed in combat.

While in Avon we met a couple that we knew back in Roxboro, North Carolina: Gaither and Joyce Crowder. Gaither had completed his twenty-five missions and was sent back to Avon as a trainer. He told me, as if I could do anything about it, not to be assigned to the Bloody Hundredth Bomb Group. He said it was the worst bomb group in England.

Of course, this was the bomb group that I eventually ended up being assigned to.

We went by train to Hunter Army Airfield in Savannah, Georgia, and picked up our plane that we would ferry overseas. It was a brand-new silver B-17. We were issued flight clothes and a new .45 pistol. I had to go to Radio School to brush up on my training. I checked out in two days. Our next flight would be to Grenier Field in New Hampshire.

While we were on our way to Grenier Field from Hunter Field, I knew we would be flying over North Carolina and I asked the pilot if he would buzz my hometown. He told me he would have to detour around Durham because of the gunnery range at Camp Butner; so, we couldn't.

While over Richmond, I went up into the nose of the plane where I could get a good view of Baltimore. I wanted to see if I could locate the Glenn L. Martin airplane plant, where I worked before entering the service. I knew it was located about ten miles from Baltimore on the Chesapeake Bay. That plant was so camouflaged that I couldn't find it.

Flying over New York City, I could see the Statue of Liberty below and the ships in the harbor.

Grenier Field was a beautiful place, with lots of tall pines; it might be the best that I had ever been stationed. At this base we received heavy wool flying clothes for the long flight to England. We were told that we would fly the northern route. This is when I realized that my dream in high school was coming true. After two days at Grenier Field, we headed for Newfoundland.

We left Grenier at 0230 in the morning. It started snowing when we departed from Grenier and was snowing when we landed at Goosebay that afternoon.

This was when I started keeping a diary beginning May 1st, 1944:

This is a rugged base with lots of packed snow that stretched out to meet the towering spruce forest. Saw some Inuit workers today; they couldn't speak English and I couldn't speak their language.

We lost one B-24 on the trip up here. I witnessed the plane go down in the St. Lawrence River. Hope they were picked up soon because it is freezing here. A cold I haven't felt before, but we are all well-clothed for this kind of environment. There are large pieces of ice floating in the bay.

We had to pull guard duty at our plane. Two crew-members each night. One night, a soldier walked out to our plane and asked Maltbie and I if he could go inside and look around. We let him go in. The first thing he did was tap on the side of the plane. He was shocked that the metal was so thin. He said that he would never go into combat with protection like that. He thought that a flying fortress would be as thick as a tank.

Behind our barracks was a log cabin that measured about twenty square feet with a dirt floor that had a hole in the center. Around this hole were stones and a couple of wooden benches. Outside the door was a fifty-gallon wooden barrel with long thin switches. I found out the purpose of those switches. About four o'clock that afternoon, I saw smoke coming from the chimney, and a short time later about twenty Inuits came out of the log cabin as naked as the day they were born.

Then they did something that hurt me to even look at: they began to beat each other's backsides with the willow switches until their rumps were red. But what really surprised me, was after ten minutes of the switching, they took off running down to the frozen bay about one hundred feet away and dived into that freezing water. I couldn't believe my eyes.

This base had very few women, just a few nurses at the hospital. While we were there, they began to ship in members from the Women's Army Corps and the men didn't like it at all, probably thought that women were replacing them so they could serve in combat.

June 4th:
We took off for Greenland today at 0510. While at Goose Bay, we were briefed on the base in Greenland. They showed us movies about this base and warned that if you didn't make it the first time landing you could just forget about pulling up and trying it again. The runway came down to a large bay and behind the base was a mountain about one thousand feet high.

You didn't get a second chance at landing at this base.

We lost one B-17 on this part of the flight. I saw several planes below on the snow. I guess all of these ran out of fuel. We saw one B-26 bomber that went down.

I saw my first polar bear below on the snow.

We had a good flight with no trouble with good weather most of the way. Our destination was Thule Air Force Base in Greenland. We landed at the base at 1845.

I wonder who named this island Greenland because this is one solid hunk of ice. There's just enough clear space around the edges to build an airfield. The bay looked about five miles across with large icebergs floating around in the bay. The base is surrounded with mountains about one thousand feet high with waterfalls. Across the bay is an Inuit village that you can barely see. We are not allowed to go over there.

The soldiers on this base had fifteen months guard duty. Greenland was an important weather station for all the operations in Europe. It was reported that Greenland even had German weathermen stationed here. Fifteen months on this place with nothing to do for excitement would cause a lot of men to go nuts. Some just couldn't take the loneliness and had to be sent back home. I read where Admiral Bird wrote that the cold weather didn't bother his men as much as the long months of darkness at the North Pole.

It is daylight all the time and it seems so strange to me to go to bed during the daylight. Some of the crew-members played cards all night long because they are not used to sleeping in the middle of the day. This is the first time in my life when I don't know when to go to bed or when to get up; it seems so strange with daylight all the time. I bet the darkness is terrible because it lasts for six months.
Don't know when we'll leave for England.
Some days the weather is beautiful but some days it is so windy we have to hold on to each other to go to the mess hall. The only way you can walk is to form long lines inside the building then go out in a line holding onto each other. The wind would blow you down otherwise.

I love to fish and was told that fishing was great. I borrowed tackle from a clerk and was told where to go. So, several of the other crew-members went with me to a large waterfall, and we caught enough cod to feed about forty men that night for supper. The mess hall cooks cleaned them for us and fried them; they were really good. I had a grand time fishing at this base. It was so easy to catch them. I even got tired; I caught so many.
I was fishing the next day behind the base hospital that was located about one hundred yards from the bay. I looked across the bay towards the Inuit village and saw something large in the water about three miles out. I first thought it might be a killer whale. As it came nearer, I saw that it was a

small boat, a kayak. It came right up to where I was fishing, and the person got out and pulled the kayak up on the shore. The person was dressed in fur and had a fur sack on their back. To my surprise I saw the person reach behind and pull a baby from the fur sack and go up to the hospital. This Inuit woman certainly had more nerve than most people to cross that bay full of ice in a small kayak with a baby strapped to her back. This must have taken a lot of courage.

The Inuits sold fur pocketbooks. I can't remember who bought them. On the way to England, after leaving Greenland, we began to smell something that reeked like an outdoor john. It was horrible. We started searching the plane for the cause of this odor and found out it was the fur pocketbooks. We threw them out the waist door. We found out later that the Inuits would skin an animal, and hang the skin on the side of the house, and urinate on them to set the hair.

Before leaving Greenland, we heard about the D-Day operation, the invasion of France...

The Unseen Hand

Chapter 5: Diary of Combat

What follows are entries of our flights logged in my diary.

(Editor's note: the italicized sections of this chapter are not from Bealer's original flight log; these represent writings from a later point in time.)

June 6th:
We left Greenland at 0845 heading for Scotland. We came in low over Ireland, and that country is a sight to behold. The grass has so many different shades of green. I saw a lot of ships, all heading for France. We arrived at Prestwick, Scotland, and turned our B-17 over to the base there. We all hoped that we could fly in combat with the new B-17.

This was a beautiful base with large oak trees all over the place. It seemed like I had been there before.

June 7th:
Left Prestwick early this morning by train. The trains are swell to ride in. They have little compartments with doors to the outside, about room for four people, and the trains run so smoothly you hardly know that you are moving. We arrived late in the day. It was a beautiful trip down to Stone, England. I saw some wonderful country as we traveled through Scotland. I had a pleasant surprise when we arrived here at Stone; I met J. B. Dunn from my hometown at this base. He was assigned to a B-24 bomber.

J. B. told me something that was hard for me to understand coming from a crew of men that he had trained with, but I accepted it and kept my mouth shut about what his crew had planned to do. He told me that they had all made up their minds and had agreed to go to Switzerland on their first mission. This was hard for me to accept but I did and remained quiet. I found out later from a letter from Nell that they did go to Switzerland and that they were living in a nice hotel in that country.

I have often thought about the odds of meeting friends in the service that you grew up with. Out of thousands in the military you would think it impossible to meet even one friend that you previously knew... but I met several while in the service and one in the oddest and worst places possible.

Unfortunately, I never met up with my brother, Lawrence, face to face, but did see him on a troop train while at Texas A.M. Nell and myself and other cadets with their wives were walking down a railroad track going to a county fair. A troop train was slowly passing by and I saw Lawrence in the window. He didn't see us; he was on his way to cadet training in Oklahoma. I met James Pentecost in a P.O.W. camp; I also met John Honeycutt at camp Lucky Strike after we were liberated. More about these two friends later... I went to high school with James and John and played football with them.

June 8th:
Went through procession again today after I went for a hike. Sure is pretty country. I like the climate: it rains a lot and I like the time off when it is raining. I miss Nell more and more. I will be glad to get a letter from her.

June 9th:
We received our rations today. Sure seems funny to get them and not have to buy them like we did in the States. Sure miss Nell. Met J. B. again today, went to a movie about England. I have a terrible cold and I hope I don't have to report to the hospital.

June 10th:
We have been given a pass, but I am too sick to go anyplace. We are leaving tomorrow for our final base, and I will be glad to stay in one place for a spell. We have been moving now since we left the States, about every two weeks, first one base, then another. Some are good bases, some are terrible. This base has more Master Sergeants than any other base that I was ever on. It is raining and I am just going to stay in the sack all day.

June 11th:
Left Stone today, at 0800 by train headed for Diss, England. Our base is near this little town about five miles away. On our trip down, we saw a lot of England and it is a pretty country; real flat land. We arrived at our base, Thorpe Abbott, at 1700.

June 12th:
Started radio school today and I wonder if I will ever stop going to school. Also had a physical today; the first in a long time. Guess everything is okay, and I can fly now. The chow at this base is okay.

Thorpe Abbott is a small village with beautiful old houses. The people are very friendly and have let the base bury our dead in the church cemetery. Our planes are parked behind their houses. We have no fences and no gates; we can come and go without a pass. It is raining today, and I now know why the English people are so pale: they don't have much sun.

I like this base and we are treated swell by the military personnel. I was really surprised when at Stone, before assignment, to be told that I would be stationed at the 100th Bomb Group. The Bloody Hundredth that Gaither Crowder back in Avon, Florida, warned me to stay away from.

We sleep in Quonset huts made of metal with two crews to a hut. When it rains, and it rains just about every day, one can really sleep with the rain hitting on the metal roof. But it also has its disadvantages. Men will come back from a pub, drunk, and pick up a handful of gravel and throw it against the metal building. When you are sleeping, this is Hell.

When I arrived at the 100th Bomb Group, we were told at a briefing that if we had any plans to quit flying to do it now and not make the first mission. Those who quit after their first mission would have to serve meals to the crews that they had trained with... at that time 25 missions were required to complete your tour of combat. If you made it, you would be sent home. At that time about two percent were finishing their required missions. Most of us didn't quit after a rough mission, we would all say that we had enough, but we didn't quit. Most of the time we would go to the bar and get drunk... ready to go again the next morning.

Before my first mission I had the worst butt chewing in my military career. I am sure it really embarrassed our pilot more than it did me. It was early in the morning and raining as usual and our briefing room was a large metal building with a tin roof, which made it almost impossible for me to stay awake. This is when I fell into trouble.
Our base commander was giving all the new men and the old a talk about important instructions while flying our first mission. He was speaking on a platform about four feet high and a light bulb was hanging over his head... there were about ten large leather chairs on the front row and we made for them because they were comfortable. The other chairs were metal.

My mistake was selecting one of the executive seats. With the rain falling on that tin roof, and the light over the commander's head, and early in the morning, I fell asleep. I heard the words, "Wake that soldier up!" and I knew I was in serious trouble. I jumped to attention and saluted. This brought on the laughter from everyone, except the commander.

He asked my name, and most embarrassing my pilot's name—who was several rows back. He proceeded to inform me that, "I don't like to waste my time giving the most important instructions that you could ever receive in your life; instructions that might even save your life, and to have you fall asleep not caring about what I'm saying."
He then told me, "Find a metal chair and bring it up front. Every time I call the name Moore, you better stand up and tell me what I just said." This happened every few minutes with everyone laughing except the commander.

This was very embarrassing to me, and I am sure to my pilot as well.

After five missions we received our air medal. We were in full dress uniforms when the commander pinned the air medal on us. He remarked to me while he pinned the air medal on my uniform,"Well Sergeant Moore, I guess you're awake now…" he was grinning.

I am sure that I must have given Lt. Scott, our pilot, the impression that I didn't care much about anything and not very serious about life. Off duty, this may have been true, but he knew while flying that I was all business, and that I did my job to the best of my ability. I did all that was required of me and more. Never missed a single mission—the real ones or the practice ones.

June 15th:
We heard today that B-29s hit Japan for the first time. Also, a new type of bomb, one that was not piloted, hit England. We called it a buzz bomb. They were sent over England from somewhere in France and had just enough fuel to reach England. London was the main target. When the fuel ran out, it would come down with a 2,000-bomb-payload that did a lot of damage. These bombs were not designed to hit military targets. They were designed to hit London.

June 16th:
They have raised the combat mission from twenty-five to thirty-five. I guess because of the short missions over France helping out the invasion. These short missions can still be very dangerous. We found out that our planes still go down because of the German fighters and the flak. Guess it will get better when the invasion reaches farther into France and we can have fighter escort. It is raining today. We heard from headquarters that the invasion is going as good as expected and that is good news. I really feel for the ground troops that are fighting. May God be with them. They have it a lot worse than we do. If we make it back, we have a nice bunk to sleep in and plenty of good food. We catch Hell in the air on a mission, but we are not in constant danger when we return. We had another red alert today and had to hit the foxhole. When we have one, we hit the foxholes right outside our barracks. Sometimes the buzz bombs will get a good tailwind, will fly past London, and will run out of fuel somewhere over England. They even go across England sometimes and land in the Atlantic. The R.A.F. (Royal Air Force) will try to shoot them down and sometimes they are successful. From our foxhole, we watched a Spitfire plane try to intercept a buzz bomb. The bomb went into a cloud, and the pilot of the Spitfire banked around the cloud; he wouldn't go into the cloud after the buzz bomb.

London is being hit harder than it was in 1940 by the Germans. The buzz bombs are doing terrible damage to London.

June 17th:
Raining today. No mission. We will receive our rations today. Still no mail from home, and I really need a letter from Nell. I miss her more each day and would like to hear from her. May God bless her.

June 18th:
I am finally through radio school and am glad this schooling is over. It seems like I have been to some kind of school my entire military career. All I do is write letters to Nell; I hope they are getting through to her. Still haven't heard from her, but I know that she is writing to me.

June 19th:
Made Technical Sergeant today and I will be sending more money home to Nell. This outfit may be called the Bloody Hundredth, but it is the best outfit in the E.T.O. (European Theater of Operations). We are called the Hard Luck Hundredth, and the other squadrons don't like to fly combat missions with us. They say we draw German fighters like flies.

June 20th:
Lt. Scott, our pilot, flew a spare mission today. It was a tactical mission; saw flak but no German fighters. Good escort by P-51 planes. They hit a target below Paris.

Haven't heard from Nell as of yet, and I am really homesick.

June 21st:
We moved down to Ipswich today. They are repairing our runway and we couldn't fly from our base.

June 22nd:
Went on a short mission today, helping out the invasion. Saw a lot of boats in the channel; saw a lot of flak but no enemy fighters.

June 23rd:
No mission today. Went bike riding with my friend Lloyd Maltbie, the top turret gunner on our crew. He is one swell guy; very easy going, and my best friend. I met his mother and father while at Avon Park. I sure did enjoy talking with

them; they are good people. They were from Adair, Oklahoma, and own a large ranch.

Maltbie is the best liked person in our crew; everyone thinks he is one swell person. He really knows his job and is very serious about keeping the plane in good flying condition.

June 24th:
Another short mission today. We went to France on a low flying mission. Helping out the invasion. I am so tired that I can't write to Nell; will write her after I have rested. The older crews went to Berlin on what is called a shuttle raid. They bombed Berlin and then went on to land in Russia. From Russia they will go on to Italy and then return to our base.

They have made arrangements with the Russians to land there rather than return the long trip back to our base. I have talked with some of the crews that made this trip and the experiences they had in Russia must have been terrible. The Russians gave them a party at the air base. They had plenty of vodka and plenty of women at the dance they gave them.

My friend told me about the dance and the women soldiers they danced with. He said some of them were very good looking, but some were rough. He said a lot of women had medals on their uniform, and when asked what they were for they would grin and not say a thing about them. He found out later that they were decorated for killing German soldiers by cutting off their penises. What a terrible way to end it all.

We often have replacement crews assigned to our base, and when they arrived, we would meet the truck to see if we knew any of the new men. This truckload was special to us because one of the new crewmen on the truck. We were surprised to see the chickenshit Corporal from the Kingman gunnery school that made us police the area, picking up cigarette butts. He had been assigned to fly five combat missions to learn about combat, so he could better train other airmen. He was still a

Corporal and we were Tech Sergeants, and we let him know it. He really took a lot of flak from us and he didn't like it at all, but he had to take it. He told us real quick that he would just be here for a short time, but little did he know that it would be a very short visit. We saw that crew he was on go down on his first mission. We felt sorry for the other men on that crew but not for him, no regrets.

June 25th:
Went back to the 390th Bomb Squad today at Ipswich. Arrived here around three o'clock. Saw some beautiful English country. We are not too welcome here. The other crews just don't like to fly with our squadron. I have already mentioned why they don't like the Bloody Hundredth Group. It does seem like the Germans single us out in combat. We have a big D painted on the tail of our plane. *I found out later, when in prison, while talking to a young ME-109 pilot, that this was not so; he said he didn't care what bomb group he was firing on; it didn't matter to him who he shot down (more about this pilot later).*

We had an understanding with the German fighters that if we were in trouble and the other planes had left us in the flight, that if we would let our landing gear down, they would come in and escort us to a German A.F. base and not shoot us down.

It was reported that one of our planes was in trouble over Germany and let their wheels down. Two ME-109 German planes came up under their wings to escort them to an airbase, and the B-17 shot them both down and made it home. Before this incident, one of our planes had ditched in the English Channel, and a German plane strafed the crewmen on life rafts. This started the feud between the Germans and our group.

June 26th:
Rained here today. No red flag flying from headquarters. No mission. We had another red alert today. The Germans really send the buzz bombs over on a cloudy day.

Played volleyball after it quit raining. No mail from home. I have found a beautiful Eskimo puppy, and he has taken a liking to me. I bring him food from the mess hall, and I have really made a friend. He sleeps on my bunk every night. Wish I could take him back with me to our base.

June 28th:
Red flag flying on the door at headquarters; so, we will fly in the morning.
We aborted over the English Channel. We had to turn back because of bad weather over the target area. Too tired to even write Nell, so I will just relax in the bunk. Getting up at one o'clock in the morning is really rough. We have heard that we are going back to our base tomorrow, and we are happy to be going.

June 29th:
The red flag is flying, so we go tomorrow morning. Got up at midnight for another mission. This one was a target deep in Germany: Leipzig. We ran into heavy flak and a lot of German planes. Bombed an oil plant there. Didn't lose any planes from our group, thank God.

June 30th:
Received our rations today and flew to the good old 349th home base. The plane we flew to our base was called Fools Rush In. It's had thirty missions. Got paid today. No mail as yet from home. Sure miss Nell and would like to know if she is ok. I pray that she is, and I love her more each day.

July 1st:
This is one happy day for me and others of the crew. We received our first mail from home. I received six letters from

Nell, and boy they are wonderful. Mail means more to us than payday. I'm thankful to know that she is doing ok and that all is well at home. I feel like I can face anything now. The letters have really helped me, and I am sure the others also.

July 2nd:
We had to get up early today for a practice mission over England. We have to do these practice missions, but we don't like to do them. We feel like it is just a waste of time to practice because they don't count on our thirty-five, the required number to finish and go home.

July 3rd:
Raining here today and no mission. Guess they will schedule us for a big one tomorrow. There is one good thing about the rain here; it gives us time to catch up on our sleep and letter writing.

July 4th:
Another mission called off today, bad weather over target area. Thinking about home today. Guess they are having a good time celebrating the Fourth. What I wouldn't give to be there with them.

July 5th:
We had another red alert today. More buzz bombs overhead. They have evacuated the children out of London now and have moved them out in the country. The red flag is flying, so we go tomorrow, weather permitting.

July 6th:
Went to France today. We were flying at 12,000 feet. This is the first time I saw anti-aircraft fire from the ground. I was looking out the window in the radio room and saw a bright flash near a patch of woods about the size of a matchbox cover. I called the pilot and was about to ask him what the flashes meant but didn't get to finish. I found out real quick what they were. The shells from those guns burst all around

us, just off the wing tips. We blasted the target. Saw one B-17 go down in flames. Counted seven parachutes from the plane. Saw two FW-190 German fighter planes go down. The P-51s shot them down.

We were just over the front lines on this mission; you could look back and see the English Channel behind us. One of our planes from our group banked off the left, then the crew started bailing out. We didn't see anything wrong with the plane. All motors were running. I saw one crew member sitting in the waist door of the plane. The plane was slowly turning towards the Channel. The crew member finally bailed out. We thought he might have been too frightened to bail. We knew the crew of that plane, and wondered if they had cleared the front lines, or if they were over the enemy lines. *I saw this crew member later in a prison camp, the one that delayed his jump, and I asked him what was wrong with the plane. He told me the inside of the plane was on fire, everything was burning, and he thought it might blow up. I told him if he had stayed just a little longer, he would have been over the English Channel. That plane slowly turned out over the Channel and went out of sight.*

July 7th:
Went to Leipzig, Germany again today. The flak was Hell. Also, plenty of enemy fighters. The target was blasted. This was a rough one. Lost one B-17, shot down by a ME-109. Sure was a long mission, eight hours on oxygen. The guy that said "War is Hell" certainly knew what he was talking about.

We saw two B-17s crash into each other. Counted eight parachutes. Don't see how any managed to escape from that crash. Eight parachutes from twenty. Sure is a sorrowful count. Don't know if more escaped or not. We were thankful to count eight chutes from that crash.
We found out later that twenty-three FW-190 enemy planes were shot down on this mission.

July 8th:
Went to France on a short mission carrying a bomb load of 4,000 lbs. Our target was an AP-bomb base (armor piercing). No loss on this one.
Received mail from Nell, sure good to hear from her, I love her.

July 9th:
No mission today, so we decided to bike to Diss, a small town about five miles from our base. We love to bike to this town and eat fish and chips; better food than we receive in the mess hall.

Sometimes the mess hall food is okay. Breakfast at our base is wonderful: two fresh eggs every morning with home fries. Flying personnel are the only ones on this base that enjoys this luxury. When we are scheduled for a mission, we eat breakfast before going. I would always place another plate over my plate so I could get four eggs instead of two. The one who was serving the eggs would be so sleepy he didn't notice the two plates... or he might not have cared that I was getting four eggs thinking this might be the last eggs ever for me.

I would make a sandwich with the two extra eggs and take it out to the crew chief that serviced our plane, like a schoolboy giving his teacher an apple, but this was a great deal more because this crew chief takes care of our plane, and this meant life or death for us. He didn't forget the kindness because he had to eat powdered eggs and they were horrible.

July 10th:
Received our first pass for London, and we were excited. This was our first visit to the city. We left by train at 0700 and arrived in London at 1200. This is one trip I didn't much care about, but London was beautiful; what was left of it. The Germans were sending buzz bombs over every fifteen minutes. Went to Piccadilly Circus and stayed in the Seaford Hotel.

July 11th:
Went on a sightseeing tour over London today. After seeing all the bomb damage to the city, I can't understand how these people can take the bombing and carry on with their lives. They have been through Hell and are facing death every day. I was walking down the street near our hotel and heard a rumble in the sky, and I knew what it meant, for we had heard this rumble at our base many times. An old woman was walking ahead of me, and she heard the sound also and stopped and asked me if that was a buzz bomb overhead. Before I could answer her, I heard the motor quit and knew the bomb was falling; so I grabbed her and shoved her into a doorway just in time before the bomb exploded about half a block away. She was not hurt, just shaken up a bit.

I left London the next day and swore it was my last trip to this city.

July 12th:
Came back to the good old Hundredth today and was glad to be back. We all agreed that we were a lot better off at our base than in London.

July 13th:
Went to Munich today. Flak was Hell. One crew went to Switzerland. We lost one B-17. Didn't see any parachutes from the plane. Saw two ME-109s go down in flames.

July 14th:
Went to Southern France today on a mission that was so secret we didn't know what we were carrying on the trip. We didn't know what the target was or what the mission was all about. It was so secret that the pilot didn't know anything about it until we were on our way in the air. I knew something was very strange because I looked into the bomb bay and saw two large bags about ten feet long and five feet high. No bombs. Not knowing where we were going and what we were carrying made this trip very exciting. We were flying so low that we

could see the tops of the houses below, and we saw smoke coming from all the chimneys on the route we were taking. *Later after the mission, we found out this was the plan for us: to follow the smoke from the houses to guide us to our target. The Free French Underground fighters were waiting for us in a large field where they had a small fire in the center. We had twelve planes on this trip and only from our Bomb Group. One plane that went was also a spare.*

We circled the field just above the treetops and came in low and dropped our bags that we were carrying. We saw a large group of men and women come running out of the field and quickly dragged the bags, then loaded them on wagons. No flak or fighters on this run. We called it a milk run: a very easy mission that we all enjoyed *(more about this mission later and why it was so secret)*.

July 15th:
I didn't receive any mail today from Nell. It is raining here, nothing to do but rest and sleep and dream of home. We received fifty dollars each today for ferrying the B-17 over here. I will send it to Nell. Thinking more of home each day; guess dad will celebrate tonight and try to forget the war. I know they are all praying for our safety.
One can feel their prayers.

July 16th:
Today is Sunday. No church for our crew. We are flying a practice mission. We don't like these practice missions. Wish they would leave us alone on Sunday, but this is war and I guess we need the practice.

July 17th:
Went to Paris, France today and the flak was heavy. We were hit under the plane. Didn't do too much damage, but we felt it. We bombed a bridge with 2,000 lb. bombs. No losses on this one.

July 18th:
Went to Kiel, Germany, to bomb a submarine base there. I have never witnessed so much flak before; the sky was black with exploding shells. That base was well protected with anti-aircraft guns. At the rate we are flying, we should be home by Christmas. We are fast completing our number of necessary missions: thirty-five are required to finish. We have a lot more to complete before we are finished.

July 19th:
Today we had our first bad luck, and a day that Lt. Scott lost his cool. This is the second time I have heard angry words from him. Most of the time he is cool and easy going. The first time he was angry was over Tampa, Fl. on that night flight to Greenville, S.C. This time it was over Germany.
We were on our way to Schweinfurt, Germany, to bomb an oil plant. We never made it. We began to lose altitude because we couldn't feather the prop. It was what we called a windmilling prop and it was shaking the plane terribly. We were, at this time, about eleven thousand feet and going down.
Our entire group had left us, and we were still over Germany. The pilot called me and told me to break radio silence and call for escort. I called in and a P-38 came along beside us. That is when I saw a German jet go under us in a fast dive. The P-38 plane went after him. *This P-38 pilot wrote an article about this incident and someone sent me this article in 1948.*
We were still losing altitude. The pilot called us on the radio, and told us to throw out everything that was not tied down. We threw out the gun barrels in our guns, all the ammunition, and all of the radio equipment except the main one. All this went out the waist door of the plane, but still we were losing altitude fast. The pilot radioed us to prepare to bail, standing by that open waist door and looking down on enemy territory was rough. We were waiting for the order to jump. There is a big difference in waiting to jump than when the plane is on fire and going down, you know the only way to survive is jump. The co-pilot pushed the button to feather the prop, and it started to run smoother and we were told to stay in the

plane. That was good news for us, but we were not out of the woods yet... we were still losing altitude.

We eventually stabilized, but we were over Germany without any firepower in the waist. We threw out all the guns. I heard Lt. Scott, the pilot, ask the navigator for a heading for Switzerland. The navigator called him back and told the pilot that we would be over Holland in a few minutes and we could land there. The pilot told him, "Don't you know the Germans have been in Holland since 1939? If we land there I'm going to kick your ass all over the place if the Germans will let me!" Then he called me and told me to break radio silence again, and send out an S.O.S. for a heading. We soon saw two P-51 fighters out of gun range give us a sign that they were coming into us. They did this by pulling up and giving us their outline so we could identify them from the ME-109 German planes. B-17s were noted for shooting anything that came into gun range. They came up under our wings; they told the pilot that we were heading deeper into Germany; they told us to turn around and they would follow us to the Channel. We dropped our bomb load in the English Channel because we were not allowed to land at our base with a full load of bombs.

When over the Channel, our base told us to land at a nearby base. We just made it over the White Cliffs of Dover and saw the landing field below. Going down the runway, the pilot called on the radio to hold on, we didn't have any brakes; the hydraulic system had been shot out. We came to the end of the runway, still with plenty of speed, so the pilot turned the plane into a wheat field at the end of the runway. We spun around and around, and that wheat field was torn up for about three acres. This put a large hole in the nose of the plane. A pole went through the nose, barely missing the pilot by about the size of a basketball. A farmer came out to where we were and demanded that we pay him for the damage to his field. Our pilot told him that Uncle Sam would pay the bill. This was a British field and soon a truck came out and picked us up and carried us to their mess hall but refused to feed us until we paid for our meal. The R.A.F. flying personnel often ate at our base and didn't pay a dime for their meal. Our pilot just happened to have some money in his wallet and paid for us to eat. When we arrived back at our base, we didn't have anything left, no clothes, nothing. Other men at the base heard that we were shot down, and they emptied the barracks of everything we had. We received most of our clothes back, but it was discouraging to know that we had men on our base that would do such a thing.

July 20th:
Went back to Leipzig, Germany, today. Bombed another oil plant. Saw flak all the way there and back. This was one Hell of a trip. Lost one motor by flak but we made it back to the base.
Received a sweet letter from Nell today. I pray that I will be with her soon.

July 21st:
We have a much-needed rest today. It is raining. Received four letters today and caught up on sleep and letter writing. When we don't fly, we sleep and write letters.

July 22nd:
No mission today. It is still raining here. I am glad because we need the rest. Have been helping Maltbie fix his bike. Hope we all get a pass to Diss today. Will write to Nell tonight. Nothing else to do but rest and write. I pray that Nell is doing ok and that I will see her soon… I think of her everyday and really miss her.

July 23rd:
Went to church today with John, Maltbie, Goff and Nelson. We heard a good sermon. Received a letter from mom, and I am happy to hear from her. Didn't receive any mail from Nell though. The letters really help our morale, but it also makes us homesick.

The Unseen Hand

July 24th:
The red flag is flying on the Headquarters door and that means we will go in the morning. We went to help out the invasion forces. Saw plenty of flak but no fighters. We saw a B-24 explode; nothing left, just a ball of orange smoke with pieces of plane going down; no parachutes were counted. Can't tell if the enemy fighters shot it down or flak. Just know that no one got out, and I pray that God will be with them. It is plain Hell to witness something like this... but War Is Hell... It is really rough when you see the plane in your own squadron go down, because you know the men in that plane, because you've trained with them and get to know them well. That's when it's really Hell.

July 25th:
Went to France today saw a lot of flak. We were flying in the coffin corner, the low group. B-17s fly in a staggered formation, three high, three in the middle and three in the lower part—the coffin corner, named so because that is the position where you catch Hell; not only from flak but also the enemy fighters pick out the lower planes to shoot down.

The lead plane has the Norden bombsight. We drop our bombs when the lead plane drops theirs. Sometimes, while flying in the coffin corner, you can look up and see the bombs hanging in the bomb bay of the top planes. The bomb run lasts about five minutes... and looking up and seeing those bombs that are ready to be let loose can put the fear of Hell into you. Sometimes the plane underneath would be hit by the bomb load. This happened to some planes. You never knew when some terrible accident would happen, and when it did happen, it usually meant death. We didn't know then about the term "friendly fire," but saw plenty of it. We didn't call it that back then. We just called it 'tough luck' and we prayed it wouldn't happen to us.

On this mission the overhead plane was hit by flak, everyone bailed out, thank God.

I feel like getting good and drunk tonight, so I might be able to forget what I saw today. These missions are beginning to tell on us.

July 26th:
These past few days have been terrible. I will never forget what we have been through, and I hope I will never see anything like this again. There is a Hell on earth and it's in the sky as well as on the ground. There is death everywhere and at almost anytime. You never know when your number is up. Planes going down in your own squadron, and you wonder who will be next. Even at base you might be killed by a buzz bomb. These come over nearly everyday but pass over us most of the time. It is believed that a buzz bomb hit a B-24 on the next base over from ours. We were waiting to take off early one morning, and we saw a large explosion over on the next base. The B-24s were taking off for a mission. I am sure no one got out of that plane alive. I am sorry for the people in London. They have been through Hell and are still going through it every day and night. They can take it, but it must be terrible for them to live in such times. I know they will be glad to see this conflict end, and peace will come again to this world.

July 29th:
Went to Meersburg today. We bombed an oil field there. We were flying in the high position today, and I thank God for that. I hope I never face anything like this mission again. Nine-man crew today—Nelson is sick with a real bad cold and cannot fly on this one. He is our waist gunner. We had a tenth crew member today—it was God. He was with us on this one, for sure. We dropped our bombs and headed for home. The radio operator has to check out the bomb bays for any bombs that didn't fall. If the bay is clear he calls the pilot and tells him to close the doors. This is the part of my job that I don't cotton to very much. It is very dangerous. Especially if one of the bombs fails to drop, and sometimes, they don't all

drop. When this happens, I have to go back into the bomb bay and kick it out.

I didn't write at all about this mission because I was too shook up to write about it… it was simply too horrible to write at the time. I looked out the window and saw a sight that I will never forget: the radio operator of another plane in our squadron was hanging under the plane with no chute on… and I knew him. We were real close to the other plane, just off the wing. We flew better this way for better firepower. The radio operator had probably checked the bomb bay, like I did, and the prop wash from the motors sucked him out. No one on his crew saw him; they had no idea what was happening. The pilot broke radio silence and called the other plane but it was too late. You could see him trying to pull himself back into the plane, but he didn't have the strength to pull himself back up. He finally let go and went down with no chute to his death. Watching him fall was Hell to witness.

July 30th:
Raining today and I am so thankful no mission today. No mail from home. I pray that Nell is doing okay. Hope to see her soon. I miss her more and more each day. Guess she is big around the middle now, and soon will be in the hospital for the blessed event; I pray God will watch over her, and that she will not have a hard time in delivery.

July 31st:
Received mail from home. Didn't have to fly last night and hope we don't tomorrow. We need the rest; we are all so tired. These missions deep into Germany really take a lot out of us. Wearing an oxygen mask for six to eight hours can be awful. At 25,000 feet the temperature is really cold, about forty degrees below zero. Sometimes, at this temperature, your gun will freeze up. You have to put a lot of grease on it. You learn very quick to take good care of your gun; your life may depend on it.

Aug. 1st:
We were decorated today with the Air medal. Full dress uniforms… Guess we are qualified airmen now. Went on a practice mission after the ceremony. The fog was horrible. We arrived back at our base, and you couldn't see the ground below for the fog. This is the worst country for fog that I have ever been in. Over the base, each plane will peel off one at a time and go down into the fog to land. I couldn't see the end of the plane's wings… this is when I wear my chute. This is the only time I wear it. I can't wear it at the radio desk or when manning my gun.

Aug. 2nd:
No mission today, and I am going to just lay in the bunk and sleep.

Aug. 3rd:
Went to a small place in France today and bombed an oil plant. Saw a lot of flak. No fighters. Didn't receive any mail today. I love Nell, and I pray she is doing ok. I pray this war will end soon.

Aug. 4th:
Went to Hamburg today. Bombed another oil plant. It was Hell. More flak than on any mission yet. We were hit a lot of times. We flew a brand new B-17, a virgin, first time in combat… it's no longer a virgin now… we made it back home. The navigator has been taken off our crew. Nelson the waist gunner is still on sick leave; sure do miss him. We flew with nine men, but an unseen hand was on board… I love Nell more everyday and I miss her.

Aug. 5th:
This is the end of my combat tour. We were shot down over Magdeburg, Germany, August 5th, 1944. The pilot, Lt. Scott and the engineer, Sgt. Lloyd Maltbie, were killed. I lost two good friends that day.

The Unseen Hand 59

Almost all of the rest of the book will be from my memory about my time as a German P.O.W. I have a few notes taken from the book that I carried while in camp and on the long march across Germany.

Sgt. Lloyd Maltbie, 1944

Read the letter Bealer wrote to Maltbie's parents in Appendix B.

Chapter 6: Premonition

I have no idea of how many people believe in premonitions, but I certainly do. Let me explain why: I believe in someone who loves us and gives us a warning to be prepared to face something in our lives.

At our base in England, we had a bar that served beer and other drinks, and sometimes they had Cokes. The first night at our base, we walked over to the bar for a beer, and they had a large book with names of the men at our base. Each soldier would list his name and hometown in the book. This was a help to everyone to find out if any men were on the base from his hometown. I was surprised to find Thomas O'Brient's name in the book, and I wondered if he was still on the base. After signing my name, I turned around to go to the bar, and I saw a large fellow at the bar. I knew this was my friend Thomas. I walked up to him and slapped him on the back, and boy was he surprised to see me. Thomas and I worked at the same plant in Roxboro before the war and knew each other as most people did in that small town. Thomas became a close friend and encouraged us before each mission.

On August 4th after our terrible mission to Hamburg, Germany, the red flag was flying on the Headquarter door, and we knew we were to go the next morning, weather permitting.

Thomas O'Brient loaded our plane with gas and bombs. He would come over to our barracks and tell us how much gas he had loaded, what bombs we'd be carrying, and when he knew we were scheduled for a mission the next morning.

The Unseen Hand

After supper, I rode over to his barracks on my bike and told Thomas what I wanted him to do for me. I said to Thomas, "I have a feeling that I'm not coming back from this mission. Please listen carefully."

He protested saying, "I don't want to hear this kind of talk."

"I know. We're not supposed to talk about stuff like this. Look, I haven't shared this with anyone on the crew. I have a brand-new pair of shoes under my bunk and a new .45 pistol in my raincoat."

I never carried my .45 with me on a mission. Our commander told us that it was our decision to carry our .45: it might save your life or it might get you killed. He informed us that the .45 had saved some crew-members' lives, but it also had caused some to be killed. He said if you parachuted down in the country, it might help to keep the German farmers away from you, and to keep them from running a pitchfork through you. *Later in P.O.W. camp, I met a crewman that had his front teeth knocked out. He parachuted and came down on a farm, and the farmer was about to run him through with a pitchfork. He pulled out his .45 and it saved his life, but when the German soldiers arrived, they took his gun and let the farmer work him over, knocking out his front teeth.*

I told Thomas, "Listen, take anything of mine that you can use, but send Nell my pipe collection and my other personal things."

Thomas agreed to do this for me, but he still didn't believe that I would be shot down.

After the war was over and I came home, I met Thomas uptown on the street and I hugged him and said, "You didn't think I knew what I was talking about that evening." He told me he was in the radio tower that day and heard over the radio that Lt. Scott's plane was going down in flames. He had a feeling that he'd never had before. He said he jumped on his bike and was the first one to our barracks. He sent everything home like he promised...

We had an all-out-effort that day: one thousand airplanes heading for Germany. Over the English Channel we test fired our guns and went on oxygen at ten thousand feet. Pop, the tail gunner, called me on the radio; he was taking pictures of the planes behind us. He called to tell me that when we got back, we would take the film into Diss to be developed. When he said those words, I knew this was our last mission. I reached down and tied my G.I. shoes to my parachute harness; something I had never done before. I was thankful I did this because when my chute opened both my flying boots flew off my feet. I still had my shoes tied to the harness. Thank God I still had those shoes.

Words cannot describe some of the terrible conditions that we went through and the horrible things we saw, especially on the three-month march across Germany. Life behind barbed wire was hard to accept at first because of the conditions in these camps. But after our stomachs became accustomed to being without food it seemed to be a little better. We were always hungry, but after the first month it didn't seem so hard. I thank God that I didn't smoke, and wasn't addicted to cigarettes, and that I had never been a heavy eater. William Nelson, the waist gunner, was not on our last mission, and this was a fortunate thing for him because he was such a heavy eater: first in the chow line and the last to leave the mess hall. He never got enough to eat. He would always carry candy bars on every mission and would share one with us, provided he had enough for himself.

The Unseen Hand

We were referred to as the Bloody Hundredth, a hard luck outfit, but we knew we were doing our job. In the outfit, next to the pilot, the radio operator was very important. I am not boasting because all the crew was important and had to work together as a crew, but if a mission was aborted, it was the radio operator who was notified. Sometimes aborting a mission was very important. Bad weather over the target was sometimes a reason, and it happened often. It was the duty of the radio operator to pick up the secret code for each mission and give it to the pilot. It was listed on edible paper and if we were forced down, it was to be destroyed by eating it. Also, we had a button on the radio that, if pushed, it would self-destruct. I didn't have to destroy the radio the day we were shot down. We were also instructed to save the bolt stud on our guns, if we had to throw out the guns. We had a Major back at our base that would always give us a talk before each mission about how important it was to save the bolt stud and to always take it out before throwing out our guns. The .50 caliber machine gun was useless without the bolt stud. We nicknamed him "Major Bolt Stud."

The Norden bombsight was always protected. It was also destructible and had to be destroyed if shot down.

We were chosen to carry over 400 tons of supplies on a mission to the freedom fighters in Southern France, July 14th, Bastille Day, and our group was honored later for this mission. But our crew was not present for the honors. We were shot down before we could receive the medal.

We did our part, but luck was not with us for the honors...

Lt. Scott & Crew (Bealer 2nd from left)

"Kaput" B.W. Moore 8.5.44

Chapter 7: Kaput

On this terrible day, August 5th, 1944, the flag was flying on the Headquarter door meaning we were to go if the weather was okay. We were awakened that morning by the one that had that duty, a duty that I would have hated. Can you imagine waking up a crew that might not come back? This person that had that awful duty was one swell guy. He had been wounded in combat on a mission and was assigned to this job, and I am sure he didn't like to wake up the crewmen for a mission. I never heard anyone gripe about being woke up by this fellow.

We would then go to the mess hall for breakfast, and it was always fresh eggs. After breakfast, we would go and pick up our parachutes. I will never forget the morning I went to pick mine up. The parachute rigger would always kid me. I remember asking him the first time I picked mine up about how to use it, and he told me if it didn't work to bring it back and he would give me another one. That morning he told me he had filled mine with sand. (When I pulled that ripcord, I thought about what he had jokingly told me.)

I went to pick up the secret code, then we all piled into a jeep that carried us to the briefing room where the base commander had a large map of the target area. He explained what the target would be and how much flak and fighters we could expect. After this, we gathered in the back room for prayer.

There is a saying that there are no Atheists in foxholes... well after your first mission it is certainly true in the air. Most everyone in each crew would go in for prayer. We were then carried out to our plane where we would unlock the box that contained our guns and ammunition. We would then place the gun barrels in our guns and load the ammunition boxes with .50 caliber machine gun bullets.

After this we would dress in our heavy flight uniforms. We would then wait for the flare that signaled us to take off. Each group was given a point to circle after take-off for getting in formation for the mission. We would have thirteen planes in our squadron; one plane went alone as a spare in case another plane had to turn back.

I have read that the Germans across the Channel could hear all those heavy bombers warming up for a mission.

After we were in formation, we would then head out across the English Channel where we would test fire our guns. This was also a dangerous part of our mission. We were flying always in a tight formation... *my good high school friend Royal Todd was killed when the planes were test firing their guns. He was hit in the chest by a .50 caliber bullet from another plane in his squadron. I didn't hear of this terrible accident until I was liberated.*

I just happened to hear from his crew members, that I didn't know at the time, speak the name of Royal, a very odd name, the only one I have ever heard... we were all in a P.X. at Camp Lucky Strike in France. I overheard their conversation and asked them if this person was from Roxboro, NC and they said yes. Then I told them I was from Roxboro and that I had gone to high school with Royal and was a close friend. Then they told me what happened to Royal. I told his crew that I would go to see his parents when I arrived home. Royal's father was a Baptist minister.

Our target this day was Magdeburg. There was a large oil plant there. This was a large city deep into Germany, very near Berlin. This city was heavily fortified with anti-aircraft firepower.

We could see up ahead the shells exploding, and the air was black. The shells were exploding at the same altitude in which we were flying. Fighters attacked us before we hit the target area. We had plenty of P-51s flying escort with us, and they dropped their extra gas tanks to start shooting down the ME-109s; our guns were also firing on them. The ME-109s left us when we were near the target.

I heard the pilot turn the plane over to the bombardier when we were on the bomb run. This lasted for about five minutes, but it felt like an hour. I heard the bombardier call "bombs away," and then he called me to check if the bomb bay was clear of all bombs. I reported, "all clear," but I didn't get to finish my call, the explosion knocked me through the door that led into the waist part of the plane.

I hit the rod that held the ball turret in the plane; I knew we were going down and I knew my chute was in the radio room under the table. I had to crawl back into the radio room. Everything was on fire. So much smoke that I could hardly see. I found my chute and snapped it on and crawled back to the waist door. I could hear the plane winding up in a spin, and it was going down fast... No one could stand up because of the force of the spin.[1]

---

[1] Account of the incident taken from the 100th Bomb Group site are as follows:

The following was quoted from Richard L. Goff's 1983 letter to Jim Brown:

"On August 5, 1944 we were on our 14th mission. Just before the target we were forced out of formation by another aircraft.
At that time we were hit by flak near the upper turret and behind the pilot. The plane began to burn. Just before being hit we had salvoed the bombs. There was a hell of an explosion and then the plane caught fire. We were at 24,000 feet. I managed to get out of the ball. The Waist Gunner and Radio Operator went out of the plane first, then me followed by the Tail Gunner. There was no bail out signal because the plane was destroyed when first hit by flak. I asked John (Eschback), who was the oldest of the crew, he was 30 and I was 19, how we ever survived getting out of the aircraft not to mention the long decent and the mad people of Magdeburg. He said training and discipline. Everything went like clockwork and no one lost their head."

Report by Lt. Edward J. Konopack adds that he and F/O Fred W. Harvey were unable to bail out because of the aircraft was in a spin but the ship blew up and they were thrown out by the force of the explosion. Probably the centrifugal force prevented Scott from getting out or he may have been killed by the initial flak hit...

ATTACHED EYEWITNESS DESCRIPTION OF CRASH, FORCED LANDING, OR CIRCUMSTANCES PERTAINING TO MISSING AIRCRAFT

A/C #42-37839, Crew #4, B-17G
"At 1252 hours A/C #839 pulled out to right or was forced out by prop wash. A/C #865 moved up to fill in the formation. Pilot Scott apparently was trying to salvo bombs. About 90 seconds before bombs away (1256 Hours) bombs were salvoed. After dropping about 75 feet all 5 bombs exploded. At the same time it was observed that #2 engine was flaming. Wings and fuselage soon began to flame and two chutes came out the waist door. The A/C continued straight and level going down on fire. It did not explode."

HEADQUARTERS
100TH BOMBARDMENT GROUP (H)
Office of the Intelligence Officer
SUBJECT: Report on T/Sgt. Lloyd E. Maltbie, 18193937
To: T/5 James P. Hill, 38182822, 34th Evac. Hosp. (SM). APO 403 %
Postmaster, New York City, New York APO 559

31 July 1945

1. All information we have at this Headquarters concerning T/Sgt. Lloyd E. Maltbie, 18193937, is as follows: He was Engineer and Top Turret gunner on a B-17 crew. His pilot was Lt. Bert L. Scott. On the mission of 5 August 1944, he was flying in A/C #639 (last three numbers). This A/C was seen to be in distress just before bombs away over the target of Magdeburg, Germany. It fell out of formation and jettisoned its bombs. Soon after that fire broke out in its #2 engine, spread into the left wing and seemed to just about cover the entire plane in a very short time. A few chutes were seen in the vicinity, but observing crew members did not know if they came from this A/C. The A/C continued down in a shallow glide and it was believed that all crew members could have bailed out. This happened at 12:52 hours. Anti-aircraft fire was intense and it is possible that Sgt. Maltbie and his pilot, Lt. Scott, were both killed in the A/C. All other members of the crew were prisoners of war and have subsequently been liberated.

2. The A/C in question must have crashed a few miles from Magdeburg, but there are no reports confirming this fact. It is possible that the battle causality office in Paris had more information. Also the Adjutant General's Office in Washington, D.C. should have further information concerning the two member of this crew who were killed. I regret my inability to give you any definite information, but trust this letter may furnish leads to the answer of all your questions.

Sincerely
Charles w. Terry
Capt., Air Corps.
P.W. Officer

Chapter 8: The Unseen Hand

This is when I felt the presence of someone helping me to the waist door. I couldn't see anyone, but I felt the presence of someone helping me that gave me strength to reach the door where I had to bail out. Jim and Pop were trying to get the door open and they were having trouble...

I reached up and grabbed the handle that we grab to help ourselves into the plane when entering, and gave the door a good kick and it flew open. I almost went out feet first but managed to pull myself back into the plane. I didn't want to go out feet first; I wanted to go out in a balled-up position.

One of the motors on the right side was on fire and the flames were shooting past the waist door. I knew I had to delay opening the chute until I was away from that fire, so I delayed in pulling the ripcord.

I saw the plane blow up under me, and I wondered if anyone from the nose made it out.

When I pulled the handle of the parachute, nothing happened, and I thought of what the parachute rigger had told me that morning–that he had filled my chute with sand. The small chute came out just a little, and I grabbed it and pulled, and when I did, that chute came out full force and burnt the Hell out of my face.

When that parachute opened, it was the most beautiful flower on earth. We were always warned to wear our parachute straps very tight on our legs, and I found out why when that chute opened. It really jerked me up, and I was so sore between my legs for three or four days. What was also very frightening, I could look down and see the parachute under me as I swung back and forth. I thought that I was going to fall back into that chute as I swung out from it. Finally, I stopped swinging, and it was so peaceful floating down through the clouds. The only sound was the small chute on top that was moving around with the wind, no noise, just the swirling of the small chute on top.

I enjoyed the ride, but not for long. I saw an ME-109 German fighter plane coming at me. When he went under me, I could see the pilot in the cockpit. The prop wash from the fighter started swinging me again, this time worse than before. I thought, this time, I was certainly going into that chute, but I soon got control again. I counted four chutes below me; I saw nine land in a river and another land in a large square space in the city. I tried to guide my chute to this spot but was lucky I didn't land in that square. We hit an oil plant and the fire was terrible. The smoke ascended about ten thousand feet and the fire was awful. I didn't want to land in that fire.

I prayed on my way down not knowing what was awaiting me on the ground. I thanked God for getting me out of that plane and was asking for Him to help me when I landed.

It was strange coming down over the city. The first thing I heard was car horns blowing below. Then I heard people talking. I remember looking up at my chute before hitting the building. It seemed the air went out of the chute at about fifty feet from the building that I hit. The building was three stories high and it joined another taller one. This building had a round slate roof that was very slick, and I started sliding down; I tried to dig my fingernails into the roof causing them to bleed but I couldn't hold onto anything.

I went over the edge and the only thing that saved me from falling three stories was that my chute fell across the chimney stopping my fall. I heard a voice in the window of the taller building asking me if a had arms. I thought he was asking me if I could use my arms to pull myself up, but he was asking for guns.

I looked up and saw my first German, face to face.

"Madgeburg" B.W. Moore

Chapter 9: Face to Face with the Enemy

He asked me "Havese arms?" I think I gave him the idea that I was armed.

I often think of what happened next. The lines of my chute fell near a window, and two or three civilians were trying to pull me up. Something seemed to tell me to stay away from that opening and not to go towards it. Had I been pulled into that spot where the civilians were, they probably would have killed me. Two Luftwaffe soldiers were let down on that slippery roof and helped me up into a large room with about twenty men. There were three Luftwaffe soldiers and one German officer and three Gestapo agents. The Gestapo men took control and stripped me down to my GI underwear.

Everything was happening so fast that I didn't see the fist that almost broke my nose. Blood shot all over the Gestapo's coat. That really made him mad, and he took it out on me by hitting me several times in the face; then he jerked my head back by my hair. I started crying because I knew this was the end. Finally, the German officer thought that I had been beaten enough, and he took control. The three soldiers helped me down the stairs... I didn't know it at the time, but my left leg was broken when I landed on the sloped roof. All the weight went on my left leg.

I didn't know what was to happen to me next when we went outside, for I saw a large crowd around the building when I was falling. I knew that I wouldn't get off with just a bloody nose and bruised face when I went through that crowd of civilians with only four soldiers to guard me. There must have been about seventy people outside waiting for me, waiting to see an American Airman that had just destroyed their plant.

The crowd was enraged, and they let me know it when they saw me come out the door. I had blood on my face and on my underwear down the front. A mother had a small child with her, and when the child saw the blood on my face, she let out a scream and then the beatings started again. The mother had an umbrella with steel flats in it, and she started hitting me over the head with the umbrella. I had no way of defending myself. I had my clothes in my arms and couldn't ward off the blows to my head. The four soldiers didn't try to help me either; they just let the civilians have their day, although they did stop the people from trying to place a rope around my neck.

The soldiers led me through the crowd to a car on the other side of the street while the crowd spit on me, and hit me several times in the face while pulling at my hair. I was thankful when we finally reached the car and we sped away from that place. I think the German soldiers allowed the civilians to get their reward by working me over, but they were not allowed to kill me, which I believe they would have, if given the opportunity.

One of the German soldiers spoke a little English, and he asked if I had eaten ham and eggs for breakfast. I laughed when he said the word "ham," he was very young, and it surprised me that he would even talk to me because most of the young soldiers were very hardcore Nazis and hated Americans. These men were friendly and offered me a cigarette.

We had about a ten-minute ride to a large civilian jail surrounded by a large stone wall with an enormous front gate of metal. They helped me out of the car and helped me over to the stone wall and told me to stand by the wall. The soldiers went inside the building. Just about that time, a squad of German soldiers came through the gate with rifles on their shoulders and were ordered to halt right in front of me. There were about twenty-four men in this group. I knew this was the end for me. I had read stories about the firing squads and watched films about executions of prisoners, and I fully expected to be shot by this stone wall.

I didn't realize that this squadron of soldiers were probably taking a lunch break... soon the order was given to fall out, and they left laughing at me as they went into the building. I almost fainted and would have had I not sat down against that wall.

A few minutes later a soldier came out to get me and led me into the building. He helped me to a room and told me to sit down. A few minutes later a German officer came into the room with a Hitler youth of about fourteen years old. When the kid saw the blood on my face and on my underwear, he jumped back in fright. This caused the officer some embarrassment. When the Hitler youth settled down, he asked me in good English where I had come from. I told him I was only going to give my name, rank and serial number. He translated this to the officer; he asked me again, this time about my squadron and where we came from. I gave him the same answer. Finally, they brought me a bowl of water and a towel to wash my face. Then I was carried into another room where I met up with Pop (S/Sgt. Daniel J. Sullivan) and Jim (Sgt. James J. Rakosnik, Jr.).

Jim was ok and he had not been beaten. I found out later, when we were left alone in that room, that Pop was the one that I had seen land in the river. It was funny how he explained what had happened to him.

He said as soon as he hit the water, he quickly unbuckled his parachute and inflated his "May West life preserver." He didn't want the parachute to carry him under the water and drown him. He said he was floating on his back and heard someone laughing on the bank. He looked up and saw a German soldier, who motioned for him to stand up. When he did, he was only in two feet of water.

We were worried about the other members on the crew, if they had made it out. We knew that Goff (Sgt. Richard L. Goff) had made it but wondered why he was not with us. We knew all had made it out of the waist of the plane, but we didn't think that anyone made it out from the upper part, toward the nose. Sullivan was a spare gunner on this flight, and he had gone up front to help the bombardier man the guns in the nose of the plane. Nelson (Sgt. William T. Nelson), the regular waist gunner was sick, and did not make it on this flight.

"The End" B.W. Moore

Early the next morning, the Germans brought in a crew member that we didn't recognize at first. It was Goff, the ball turret gunner. He was the parachutist I saw land in the large cement square in the middle of town, the one that I wanted to land in, but thank God I didn't. The Gestapo headquarters was located in that block. They were waiting for Goff and grabbed him before he even hit the ground. They hauled him into a room and beat him all night. His face was so black and blue and swollen that we didn't know him. Both of his eyes were black, and his mouth was swollen.

Goff was only seventeen. He lied about his age; no one was allowed to go overseas this young or even join the armed forces at this age. The pilot found out about his age before we left the States. His mother knew a congressman, and this kept him on our crew. The congressman knew a lot of important people in Washington that made it possible for him to remain with us.

The next morning, they fed us breakfast; just a piece of buttered bread and a cup of hot tea. The Germans brought the co-pilot (F/O Elmore W. Harvey) and the bombardier (2nd Lt. Edward J. Konopak) into our room. The co-pilot said that they were blown out the front of the plane. They didn't know if the top turret gunner or the pilot had made it out or not.

About two o'clock on Sunday morning, a young German Luftwaffe pilot came into our room. He was dressed in a beautiful blue uniform and he spoke perfect English. He told me he received the credit for shooting us down, and he gave me a newspaper that showed our plane going down in flames.

I was the only one that would talk to him. He didn't try to question us about our mission, he just wanted to be friendly and talk to us.

We found out from him that Maltbie and Lt. Scott had been killed. He told me to look out the window below, and I could see their bodies under a canvas tarp on a truck bed that was parked below the window. The tail section of our plane was also on the truck bed. He asked me if I would like to go down to identify the bodies. I told him that I didn't want to go. He seemed to understand and told me where they would be buried in Magdeburg.

He congratulated me on our Air Corps and then asked me what was the worst target that I had been over. I told him probably the sub-base in Kiel, Germany. I didn't think that I was giving him any information that he could use.

He then told me that they didn't have a city anywhere in Germany that could send up as much anti-air fire as London. He said that it was Hell to fly over that city. I am sure he knew what he was talking about. He talked to me about two hours then he left. He wished me good luck and he seemed to mean it.

We were not given anything to eat all day except breakfast. Late in the evening, they brought us four loaves of bread, one for each of us. We had never seen any bread like this and wondered if this was some kind of joke the Germans were trying to pull on us. This "so called bread" was covered in sawdust and was almost black in color. It was the worst tasting bread. No one could eat it, and we just threw it on the floor.

Later that night we were told that we would be leaving around four in the morning for Frankfurt. I asked the officers what we should do with the bread when we were leaving, and they said to leave the damn stuff, no one would eat it anyway. I told Pop that I thought we should take the four loaves with us. He agreed, since we didn't know when we would get anything else to eat.

Pop and Jim helped me onto the train. The station was empty of all but a few civilians, and the German guards wanted it this way for they didn't know what would happen if the civilians found out that we were the airmen that destroyed their oil plant on Saturday.

The next morning on the train to Frankfurt we were in a compartment with other enlisted men, the officers were in another compartment separate from ours. The German guards opened their nap sacks and brought out some bread, not like ours, and sliced a few pieces then they put butter and jam on the slices and started to eat. When we saw them do this it made us hungry, so we borrowed his knife and we sliced some of our bread, by this time it tasted like chocolate we were so hungry. I had saved the four loaves, and there was plenty for us, but soon the door opened, and a German guard came in with the co-pilot. He asked me if I had any of that bread left. We reluctantly gave him a loaf.

The trip down to Frankfurt was beautiful. On our way we passed a Ford Motor Company factory and it was operating full blast. We saw plenty of Ford trucks. We wondered why this plant was still in operation... why hadn't it been destroyed... (After three weeks of interrogation, we came back this way and at some distance from the plant we noticed how the tracks became very bumpy and we saw large holes alongside the track. When we came to the plant, we didn't see anything but smokestacks; the Brits had completely destroyed it. We went by very slow, and when the civilians saw us, they started throwing bricks. I am glad we didn't stop.)

We arrived at night in Frankfurt, and we were quickly carried through the railway station. It had several large holes in the roof from recent bombings. The guards knew that the few civilians inside the station would try to kill us, so they rushed us through the station. Jim and Pop carried me, one on each side of me, and we made it to a truck parked close by.

The Unseen Hand

"Solitary Confinement" B.W. Moore

Chapter 10: Interrogation

At the Interrogation Center we were led down a hall with small doors on each side. Each door had a window covered with wire. There were rooms on each side of the hall, and it must have been fifty or more rooms in this one hall. I was shoved into a room, and the guard locked the door. This room was about four feet wide and about eight feet long. I could only lie down one way. There was straw on the floor and no bed. One light hung from the ceiling. I had no one to talk to, nothing to write on, and nothing to read. I could only sit and listen to the guard wailing down the hall. I had no idea how long I would be in this Hellhole. Or how long I could hold out before telling them what they wanted to know.

My leg was giving me Hell by this point; it was very swollen and had a large cut that was getting infected. I thought I had cut it when I bailed out but found out later I had a piece of steel in my leg from flak.

Two days went by in that cage. The only time I was let out was to use the john once a day. If I had to go before that time, I had to do my business in the straw. This was in August and the heat in there was horrific; no windows and no air circulating. I had nothing to write with or no one to talk to, so I just occupied my time by catching flies and inserting straw up their ass, and then watched them fly around the room. I had plenty of straw and plenty of flies.

I was served one slice of bread with jam and a cup of tea in the morning. In the afternoon I had a thin cabbage soup with another slice of black brot (bread). For supper I had a bowl of watered-down potato soup with a slice of bread.

On the third day, I was carried up to the German Interrogation Officer for questioning. I had already been given a slip of paper with the questions concerning where I had trained in the States, where my current base was located, how many missions I had been on, where I was born... I only wrote my name, rank and serial number on the paper. The Interrogating Officer offered me a cigarette, which I refused, telling him that I didn't smoke. He then asked me why I refused to answer the questions. He continued by saying that if I didn't cooperate that I wouldn't receive any medical attention. If I did cooperate, I wouldn't have to suffer, and my wounds would be treated. No information, no medical attention.

I was carried back to my room. Another week went by and by this time my leg was giving me pure Hell. Another week went by, and I was finally taken to a hospital where a doctor told me he couldn't put my leg in a plaster cast because there was a short supply, and these were reserved for the German troops. He ended up treating the flak wound and bandaging my broken leg very tight. When I saw the conditions of all the other P.O.W.s in that hospital, I felt ashamed for wanting medical attention so desperately.

One of the airmen in that room was so horrible to look at. He had been burned about the face with an outline of his aviator goggles. Another P.O.W. was covered with infected sores all over his body. He had been in the French Underground after being shot down, and the Germans found him in civilian clothes. He had no dog tags for identification. The doctor refused to treat him and told him he was to be shot for being a spy.

During my last week of solitary confinement, I was carried back to the Interrogation Officer. He asked me if I wanted to know any information about any of my flying companions. I asked him when he thought the war would be over. That was a mistake. He backhanded me, almost knocking me out of my chair. He said to me, "You damn Americans are never serious!" He then proceeded to tell me all about my training while in the States: where I trained, when I left, where I was stationed, what bomb group I was in, the name of my base commander, how many missions I had been on and the targets. Then he asked me if I would like to know how he got this information. He said, "Do you remember when you graduated Radio School?" I said "yes." He continued, "Your hometown paper writes all about you. We buy all the newspapers from other neutral countries and find information in them."

My father worked in a plant, and his foreman had property in Germany. He and his wife were from Germany. I found out after I arrived home that he told my father that about a week after I was shot down, he was listening to his short-wave radio and heard the Germans give my name and that I was a P.O.W.. The telegram had not been sent home at this time, so my father didn't believe him. The telegram came about two weeks later stating that I was missing in action over Germany.

Bealer's P.O.W. photograph

The Interrogation Officer told me he knew all about our crew, but he didn't know where I was born. I told him where I was born, and then he wished me luck and said that I would be out of the box in a few days. (The first time that I met him he said that I would be in that box for one month if I refused to talk.)

The next day I was taken out into the yard where I met Jim and Pop Sullivan and Goff. That was one happy day for all of us to be out in the fresh air and the sunshine. It was almost like being set free. We were all laughing and talking, asking others around us what state they were from. There must have been four or five hundred of us in that compound.

I was told that there was another P.O.W. in that compound who was from Asheville, North Carolina, and that his name was Rex Hayes. So I went over to the other barracks and found him. I especially wanted to find Rex because my mother was kin to the Hayes in western North Carolina. She was born in Roaring River. Rex and I became good friends, and we were together most of the time after that.

Rex was in terrible condition when I first met him. He couldn't have weighed over one hundred pounds. He looked like he had been starved for months and that caused me to ask him how long he had been in prison and why he didn't weigh more than he did... He was about six feet tall with red hair. He told me that he had been shot down over France in 1943. The French Underground hid him with two other men of his crew. They separated the three, and hid them in homes in the mountains of Spain. They waited until spring to take the three airmen over the mountains because of the snow. While climbing the mountains, they were captured by a German patrol.

Rex was carrying in his wallet a French note as a souvenir; the money had a picture showing a man ringing a bell. Someone had cut the bell from the money and replaced it with a picture of Hitler's head. It looked like Hitler was being hung. When the soldiers found the money in Rex's wallet, they nearly beat him to death. He was turned over to the Gestapo and they also nearly killed him.

Rex's red hair caused him to be singled out from the other prisoners, and wherever he went, the guards would point him out and he would be beaten again.

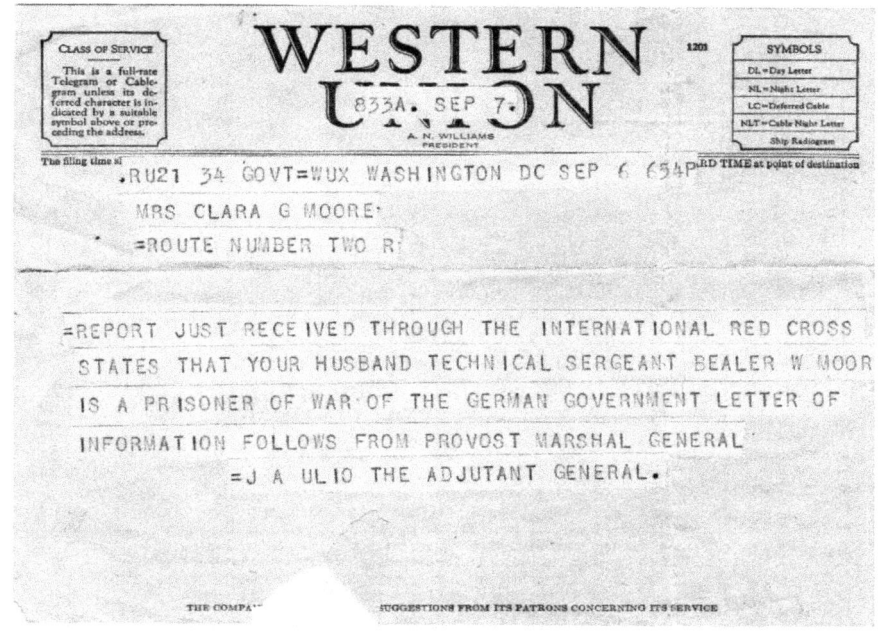

Telegram dated 7 Sept. 1944 to Nell Moore informing her of Bealer's P.O.W. status.

WAR DEPARTMENT
THE ADJUTANT GENERAL'S OFFICE
WASHINGTON 25, D. C.

v/mc

IN REPLY REFER TO:
AG 201 Moore, Bealer W.
PC-N ETO158

22 August 1944

Mrs. Clara G. Moore
Route Number Two
Roxboro, North Carolina

Dear Mrs. Moore:

    This letter is to confirm my recent telegram in which you were regretfully informed that your husband, Technical Sergeant Bealer W. Moore, 13,121,816, Air Corps, who has been reported missing in action over Germany since 5 August 1944.

    I know that added distress is caused by failure to receive more information or details. Therefore, I wish to assure you that at any time additional information is received it will be transmitted to you without delay, and, if in the meantime no additional information is received, I will again communicate with you at the expiration of three months. Also, it is the policy of the Commanding General of the Army Air Forces upon receipt of the "Missing Air Crew Report" to convey to you any details that might be contained in that report.

    The term "missing in action" is used only to indicate that the whereabouts or status of an individual is not immediately known. It is not intended to convey the impression that the case is closed. I wish to emphasize that every effort is exerted continuously to clear up the status of our personnel. Under war conditions this is a difficult task as you must readily realize. Experience has shown that many persons reported missing in action are subsequently reported as prisoners of war, but as this information is furnished by countries with which we are at war, the War Department is helpless to expedite such reports. However, in order to relieve financial worry, Congress has enacted legislation which continues in force the pay, allowances and allotments to dependents of personnel being carried in a missing status.

    Permit me to extend to you my heartfelt sympathy during this period of uncertainty.

Sincerely yours,

J. A. ULIO
Major General,
The Adjutant General.

War Department's letter to Nell regarding Bealer's P.O.W. status, dated 22 Aug. 1944.

"Japs" B.W. Moore

Chapter 11: Sankt Wendel

We were put on a train, and we left Frankfurt for southern Germany. We traveled through gorgeous country; the train ride was wonderful with breathtaking scenery; we saw some elegant castles on the way to Sankt Wendel. We arrived in a small town located in the mountains of Saarland next to France. The camp was located on top of a large mountain over-looking the small town of Sankt Wendel. We could look across the rolling hills and see sheep grazing on the hillside about five miles away. It was the first of September, and the weather had already turned cool. It was so peaceful here in this part of Germany.

We had open barracks—a long shed about two hundred feet long with open sides in the front. No windows or doors. There were no guard towers around the wire fence. It just didn't seem like a prison at all, and we were hoping that we would stay here, but it didn't turn out that way. We could hear guns being fired down in the valley, and wondered why this place had not been bombed, but we didn't have long to wait for this to happen. About four days later, we heard the sirens sounding down in the valley and we knew we were going to get our wishes granted. The German guards made us go inside the barracks, but they couldn't close any doors. We could hear the bombers coming over the town. We heard the bombs falling and knew what they were after—the gun plant below. We were so close that we felt the shockwaves from the bombs as they thundered. We couldn't show any excitement about what we heard; we couldn't shout, but the guards knew we were happy and excited about the raid.

We sure didn't hear any more guns being tested from below.

It was at this camp that I saw my first Japs. About five Japs and five German officers were dressed in striking uniforms as they walked by the outside wire. The Japs were dressed in white uniforms, very beautiful with long swords hanging down their sides.

One of the prisoners, I have forgotten his name, was from Salisbury, NC, and had been wounded in the buttocks. His butt looked like a flour sifter from all of the shrapnel. Every day he would go outside in the warm sunshine and bend over on all fours so his friend could sit behind him, and with a pair of tweezers, pull the small pieces of steel from his butt.

When the Japs and Germans passed by and saw this action going on, they nearly rolled on the ground laughing. They doubled over, and I think the Japs would have rolled on the ground had it not been for their white uniforms. This made the two prisoners very mad, and they called the Japs every name under the sun. I heard curse words that I had never heard before. They even called them slant-eyed bastards.

I don't think the Japs could understand English for they probably would have shot them.

We stayed at this camp for about two weeks. We left by train for Poland, but this train ride was entirely different from all the other train rides... it was just plain Hell.

This train ride to Poland was the worst experience that I had faced so far and one that I will never forget. We were loaded into boxcars that were called "forty and eight." This would have been just the right size for forty men and eight horses, but it didn't work out that way.

There were three sections to each boxcar. A German guard had the middle section, and each end of the car was sealed off with barbed wire. They loaded about thirty-five men into each section. It was so crowded that no one could stretch out and be comfortable. They had straw on the floor and that helped some, but the crowded space was the worst part. At each end of the car was a window that had barbed wire over it, but no windowpane, and this is where I managed to reach. The only comfort in this boxcar was when we were moving. The door where the guard was standing was left open, and we could get air from those doors. No one was allowed out, and when we had to urinate or had a bowel movement, we had no place other than the straw. The stench in that car was horrific. Some of the men had diarrhea. It was almost unbearable. We had no idea where we were going or for how long we would be in that car.

After two days and nights in this boxcar, we pulled into the marshaling yards of Berlin. About three o'clock in the afternoon a German hospital train slowly pulled out and went by us. We saw wounded German soldiers in the cars, and they were really shot up. Some in casts and some had bandages all over them. We didn't have any sympathy for these soldiers and we were happy to see them in this condition.

Of course, this was a big mistake, and one that we suffered for: as the train went by slowly, a hospital worker threw a bucket of urine and human waste right into the window where I stood. I didn't see this coming and had no time to duck. The waste covered us in the car. The guard would not give us any water to wash this mess out of our hair, and the other men in the car were cussing us for causing this terrible accident. We nearly went crazy because we had no way to wash this terrible sludge from our bodies.

That night, a plane flew over and dropped a flare that lit the whole area up so bright that you could read a newspaper in that boxcar. We knew then what was going to happen. The R.A.F. did not bomb like we did, they bombed at night: the lead plane would drop flares to light the target area; then one by one, the bombers would, in single file, drop their bombs on the target. The air raid sirens went off, and the next thing that really caused us fear was the German guards leaving for the air raid shelters, and locking all the doors behind them, thus leaving us out in the marshaling yards. We knew that if they bombed the marshaling yards, we were done for. We would be killed by the bombs or burn to death in the boxcars. There was nothing we could do but pray.

Thank God they bombed the station and not the yards. We could feel the shock from the bombs about five miles away. Every time a bomb would hit, the car would bounce. This lasted about one hour. We were locked up all night.

The guards came back early the next morning to unlock the doors, and they seemed disappointed that we didn't get bombed.

I have since read that Hitler gave order to place P.O.W.s around the marshaling yards to keep the Royal Air Force from bombing the yards.

Our train left the area of Berlin that morning. I was standing by the window looking out. After we had been traveling for about two hours, the train was going around a long curve, and I could see up ahead the train engine. I saw the engineer jump from the cab of the engine, and wondered what was going on. I didn't have long to wait. I looked to my left and saw a P-38 diving on the engine with tracers coming from its guns. I saw the engine blow up, and we came to a sudden halt. There was a river along side the railroad track, and when the guards opened the doors to let us out, I made for the river and dove into that water. I didn't care if the guards would shoot me; I had to get that filth off me, and the others were right behind me.

That was the best bath I have ever taken. I had no soap to wash with, but I didn't care; I just wanted to get that mess off. They finally hooked up another engine, and we were on our way again. I didn't get back to the window this time but managed to find a place near the door of the boxcar where the guard was sitting.

The guard this time was an older man and could speak a little English. We went through a very large town. He pointed to some large smokestacks that had gray smoke coming out of the tops of them. He told me the smoke coming from those stacks were Jews that were being cremated.

"Arrived at Stalag Luft IV" B.W. Moore

Chapter 12: Stalag Luft IV

We travelled all that day until late in the evening, finally coming to a camp located in Tychowo, Poland. I didn't know it at the time, but this was considered the worst P.O.W. camp in Germany or Poland. It was located near the Baltic Sea and near the town of Szczecin.

The German guards that met the train were from the camp and each had a leash with two German Shepherd dogs. They were so vicious that they even tried to bite the guards holding them. Several of the P.O.W.s were attacked on the march to the camp. Everyone but the wounded was made to run the distance to the camp, about three hundred yards away. The wounded were marched to the camp, but we were treated very rough. I was pushed down several times, but fortunately I was not hurt.

This camp had four large compounds about the size of a city block. Each compound had about three hundred men or P.O.W.s. Each block had eight barracks and two latrines. In the middle of the block was the mess hall. About twelve men slept in the mess hall and cooked the meals. There was one main gate, and a guard was stationed there night and day. Each corner had a "goon box," or guard tower, with two guards, a machine gun, and a large spotlight. Around each compound was a high barbed wire fence with a warning wire about ten feet inside the wire.

These buildings were made of wood and were about three feet off the ground. The front door had a glass window and the back door as well. They were locked when the shutters were closed. The lights were cut off at ten o'clock each night.

Our barracks had a long hall with rooms on each side. Six rooms in the hall that held twenty-five men. One window to each room with no glass, just shutters that were closed at sundown. The room had one large table and four chairs, a small wood stove, and one light that hung down from the ceiling. Each room had triple bunk beds with no mattresses, just straw.

No one was allowed out at night for any reason. If you had to go to the toilet during the night, you did it in a bucket in the washroom. In the washroom, we had to shave and bathe in cold water. When the weather became even more frigid in November, we suffered.

We had roll call twice each day regardless of weather conditions. One in the morning and one about five in the evening. The food had very little sustenance and very little to go around. Breakfast was one slice of bread with jam and a cup of lukewarm tea. Lunch consisted of one slice of bread with a bowl of cabbage soup or sauerkraut. For supper we always had a bowl of potatoes without any salt or butter.

About every week we received a Red Cross food parcel that was divided between two men. The food parcel contained two chocolate bars, one small can of condensed milk, a small pack of sugar, a small can of cheese, a pack of powdered eggs, one pack of cigarettes, and a small can of corned beef. No one could gain any weight from this food, but we were thankful for the parcels. Although some weeks we didn't receive any at all and we really missed the food.

We were given very little soap and just one razor blade. I had a very light beard at this time and didn't have to shave very often. We tried to stay clean, but it was terrible to bathe when the weather turned cold, and in 1944 the weather was terribly cold.

"Lost Dreams" B.W. Moore

Body lice were impossible to destroy and caused us all kinds of trouble. Men would break out in sores from scratching at night, and there was no way to get rid of the lice. Every day we would search the seams for lice eggs and would wash our underwear, but we had no hot water to help kill the lice. Even if we could, the straw was full of them. It was miserable but you managed to deal with it.

We were issued eight lumps of coal each day. These were about the size of a brick, and we would not build a fire until night. During the day we would walk and exercise in order to stay warm.

We had a visit from the Red Cross Organization in November. The German Captain in charge of the camp wanted to impress the representative from the Red Cross, so he gave us soap and hot water to clean ourselves. They wanted us to look good and clean, but they couldn't fool the representative for we were all underfed and looked starved. There was no way they could fatten us up, and the representative knew what conditions we were in. We were not allowed to talk to him.

They did release some of the P.O.W.s that had T.B. and other diseases in exchange for some German P.O.W.s. This was a happy day for the exchanged prisoners, but sad in another way. The ones leaving were leaving some of their buddies and were thinking about the ones left behind. Although they were getting to go home, it was still sad for them.

Life behind barbed wire was Hell. We were not physically harmed, other than a kick now and then from a guard, but they had other ways to make life miserable for us.

Roll call was one way that they used to make it horrible for us. We would fall out in front of the barracks for roll call, and the guards would take a count. If the count did not tally, they would count again.

Some days it would snow or rain and they delighted in making us stay out longer. They never got the right count. If one was sick and stayed in the barracks and didn't tell the

"Durnas & Berry & Rex: A Friendly Game Before Lights Out" B.W. Moore

person in charge of that barracks, then the count would be wrong, and we would have to stay out longer.

We made a deck of cards from the Red Cross boxes, and we played cards each night until the lights went out. Then we would hit the sack and sing. We had a prisoner from Alabama that had a beautiful voice, and he knew all the country western songs. He belted like the lead singer on the Sons of the Pioneers, and knew all of their tunes. We would all join in, and we really looked forward each night to hearing him sing.

Wednesday night was prayer meeting night, and Rex Hayes was the speaker and teacher. He knew the Bible and could explain the verses. Rex was a good Christian boy, and everyone liked to hear him teach the Bible.

I won a book in a raffle, and this helped me to pass the time by sketching scenes during the day.[2] I hid this book when we had an inspection of the barracks. The Germans would often pull a sneak inspection, and I would throw the book out the window when they would come into the front door. I had some poems in the book that I didn't want the guards to see. If they had found them, I would have been in trouble.

Another thing the Germans would do was to pull a sneak inspection during the middle of the night. They would come into the barracks and order everyone out into the hall, then they would go into each room and throw all the straw into the middle of the floor and leave the barracks and cut the lights out. We had to sleep wherever we could because our beds were all over the floor. No one was allowed out at night after the doors were locked, and the windows were closed.

We had a roommate that could speak German, but he insisted that we never told anyone, especially the Germans. We never knew which guard could speak English, and we didn't try to find out.

If a guard could speak English, he would never let you know that he could. They would never carry on a conversation with us. They didn't trust anyone; not even their own buddies. They let you know who had the gun and that they were willing to use it.

Some of the guards were proud to be Nazis and would let you know it. True to the Fatherland and to Hitler. Some guards were too old for combat, and some were wounded and unfit for combat. Others would get well from their wounds and be sent back to the front lines. You could almost tell which front they had served in combat. If they served on the

---

[2] Editor's note: These are the sketches used throughout the memoir.

Russian front, they would have something missing from their bodies, an arm, a leg, or eyes.

Life was not dull when there were four or five hundred men in a compound. Some odd things would strike us as funny, though most of the times things were not so funny.

We had two outdoor toilets in each compound. One day at roll call we were standing at attention while the guards counted the men. A German guard came through the main gate riding a wagon. Driving the wagon was a Russian P.O.W. There were two horses pulling a large tank loaded on the back of the wagon. This tank was about ten feet long and five feet high. The tank was used to clean out the toilets.

We were standing about thirty feet from the outdoor john. The young Russian placed a large hose into the toilet hole, then he came around to the tank and opened a gas valve on the side. The guard was on the other side of the tank, and he couldn't see what the Russian was doing. The Russian had human waste all over him, on his boots and clothing. He looked at us and winked, grinning he struck a match to the cup on the side of the tank, and when he did that tank blew the lid off, and human waste went all over the guard and all of us who were close by. The horses then bolted and ran for the gate.

The German guard caught the young Russian and knocked him down with his riffle. He kicked him several times on the ground, and I believe he would have shot the young man if we had not been there. Everyone was laughing, even the guards taking the roll call.

Our barracks were about three feet off the ground. The guards would crawl under the barracks to inspect the ground to see if we were digging a tunnel. We would let them get under the barracks then we would have a square dance in the barracks. With all that stomping on the floor, the guards would be covered in dust. They wore white coveralls, and they would come out from under the building just filthy.

I never received but one cablegram from home, never a letter, but that cablegram was wonderful news to me. I could write Nell and my family, but we doubted if they were getting through to them. Some prisoners who were behind barbed wire for two or three years did receive mail and parcels from home. Sometimes they would receive cigarettes and would keep them with them at all times; they were very valuable.

Nell made an agreement with Tampa Nugget Cigar Company to send me a box of cigars monthly, but they never reached me. When I arrived home, they sent me notice that they were being returned to them, and they wanted to know if I would like to have them. You couldn't find any cigars at that time, so I wrote them to send them on.

In camp sometimes a P.O.W. would receive a Dear John letter. You can imagine what this would do to a prisoner. One P.O.W. received such a letter telling him that his wife had divorced him. He ended his life by walking across the warning wire, and the guards on the tower shot him.

Another P.O.W. received a hand-knitted sweater with a note in it. He had been in prison for several years. He wrote her a letter thanking her for the sweater. He received a letter from the woman who knitted the sweater, and she was upset because a P.O.W. had received the sweater. She wrote that she had sent the sweater to someone on the front lines fighting. He became very angry and made the remark "How in the Hell did she think I became a P.O.W.?!" He threw the sweater away.

Life in this camp was very hard to bear but all of us depended on one another, and I never saw a fight among the men in this camp. We didn't have much happiness, but sometimes things would happen that made us laugh.

I spent a lot of my time cutting hair. I had one pair of scissors and a comb, and did a decent job. The men didn't complain too much.

Jim, the waist gunner, Pop, the tail gunner, and I were together in the same room. Rex Hayes and the other two men of his crew were also in the same room with us. Rex was our Chaplain in this barracks. We depended on him for our spiritual blessings. He knew the Bible, and he also knew how to help someone who was depressed. He suffered with backaches from where the Germans had beat him, but he never complained about his condition. He was always in pain, but nothing could help relieve it.

The only sickness that I had, other than diarrhea, was a very bad cold while in the camp. I cut a lower wisdom tooth that nearly drove me mad from pain. The only relief I could get was to bite on a spoon while trying to make the tooth come through the gum. This was all my fault because of my fear of the dentist. At every base in the States, a dentist would examine me, and he would write me out an order to report and have my wisdom teeth extracted. Army dentists were noted for their roughness, and it was just another job to them. They had no sympathy for the ones they worked on. I would tear up the order and would not go to have them extracted. I knew that I would not be on a base more than a month or two. The Air Corps had an order that no one going overseas to fly in combat could go over with his wisdom teeth. They had to come out. When I arrived at our base in England, the dentist examined my teeth, and asked me how in the Hell did I get over here? I told him that I had orders to have them extracted, but I would tear them up. He then told me that he couldn't extract them, but he hoped to Hell that I would never be shot down. He said wisdom teeth were subjected to going bad and they often did. He was right, and I paid for this stupid mistake. I begged someone to split my gum with a razor blade, but no one would do it. The Germans would not treat anyone unless it was a life or death situation. It took three days for that tooth to come through. My leg hurt nothing like this.

December was a horrible month. It snowed almost every day, and we had a foot of snow on the ground. We had men in our camp that knew how to make a radio from practically nothing, and we could hear the BBC everyday. Each morning a P.O.W. named Herb would come around to our barracks and tell us the news they had received from the radio. In December, this news was very bad because we thought the Germans were winning the war. We knew something was wrong because of the actions of the guards; before December, they were very mad all the time and hateful to us. In December things seemed to be better for them; they would laugh and joke with one another and were cocky. We found out about the Battle of the Bulge, and this was terrible news for us. For about two weeks we thought we would never be liberated and that the war was going in their favor. About every week a new P.O.W. would arrive in our camp who had just been shot down, but they seldom knew anything that was going on at the front.

Our German captain went home for Christmas leave, and he was nearly killed while at home when his house was bombed. He lost his wife and daughter in the air raid and was wounded himself. He was very angry when he returned to our camp and made life miserable for us. He had been in combat before and lost his left arm and couldn't fly anymore. He was a fairly decent man before his leave, but when he returned in late January he was a monster.

"Stalag Luft Captain" B.W. Moore

"French Saboteurs" B.W. Moore

Chapter 13: Christmas Eve

Each night after the lights were turned out, I would go to the end of the hall where the door with the window was, and I would look out at the falling snow and pray, looking in the direction that I thought was home.

On Christmas Eve, I stood looking out the window and had myself a pity party thinking about home. Christmas at our house was always special, and I was thinking about my wife and my family. I could see the snow falling from the light under the guard tower. We had the barracks next to the tower in the corner of the compound. The road came right by our barracks about forty feet away.

I saw a sight that I have never forgotten and never will. I heard men groaning and saw a group of them walking alone on the snow-covered ground. Some of them were on a makeshift sled pulled by other men; some were being helped along by their comrades; some had their feet wrapped up in rags that were covered in blood.

I watched these men as they struggled along. Tears rolled down my face as I watched the last of the men go by. I estimated about two hundred men were in that group. I didn't see but four or five guards with them, and the guards looked like they had been through Hell as well. This was the most pitiful group of men I have ever seen and probably will never see the likes of again. We found out the next day that they were captured French Freedom Fighters that had not been executed but were being used as slave labor in different parts of Germany.

We asked the Germans if we could share our food with these men, but they refused, saying they would eventually be shot, and they didn't care if they starved to death. They were placed in an empty compound next to ours. We tried to throw food to them, and some pieces of bread would fall between the warning wire. These men would try to cross the wire to get to the food, and the guards would fire at them from the tower. We had to quit for fear that they would be killed. They were marched out the following day, and I don't know if the Germans fed them while they were in our compound.

The twenty-four men in our room had made a bet that the war would be over by Christmas. We didn't have anything to bet with, so we decided that the losers would shave their heads, that is, if we could gather enough razor blades to do this. Twelve decided that the war would be over, and if not, on Christmas Eve we would shave our heads if we lost. I was one of the twelve that lost the bet. We managed to find enough razor blades; so on Christmas Eve the other twelve went to work on our heads.

The next morning, we were gathered around the stove, seven or eight of us, when the door opened, and a German guard looked in the room, he grinned at our shaved heads. He said something like 'crabs'… we didn't understand him at first, then he made the motion with fingers that he was crushing crabs. We started laughing when we knew that he thought we had crabs and had to shave our heads to get rid of them.

We felt so clean with shaved heads that the other men in the room shaved their heads too. It was the best thing that we could have done for our health. Months earlier, when the Red Cross Inspection Team notified the Germans that they were coming to our camp, the Germans decided to give all the

"Lost Bet" B.W. Moore

P.O.W.s a haircut and started at the front of the barracks cutting each prisoner's hair. At that time, we didn't want our hair cut even though it would have been best for our health. We went out the backdoor and filled our hair with sand. When the Germans started cutting our hair, the clippers wouldn't cut with the sand in our hair, so they quit, not knowing what we did. They couldn't figure out what was wrong. After shaving our heads in December, we knew that we should have let them shave our heads much earlier.

Christmas Day was a very sad day for us. The food was the same, nothing different. None of us felt like eating because of the Frenchmen in the other compound who were without food and were barely alive. I am sure we were all thinking about home and the meal our families were having this day. Each of us would tell how we celebrated this holiday and the kind of food we would have. The men from our barracks were from all over the United States, and each had a different story to tell. We decided to have a prayer meeting and asked Rex to give us a talk and to pray for us and our families. I have the prayer that Rex gave to us that morning and I cherish it and read it often... This is the prayer Rex prayed on Christmas morning, 1944 taken from my sketch book:

Some day yuletide bells will ring merrily again:

"We beseech thee our kind heavenly Father to bless us this Christmas day, Christ's birthday.

Someday Yuletide Bells Will Ring Merrily Again

Devotional Service Given on Christmas Morning By - Rex Hayes Morning December 25, 1944

Prayer: We beseech Thee our kind heavenly father to bless us this Christmas day, Christ's birthday. We thank Thee oh Father for Thou son who was born on this day two thousand years ago, fulfilling the prophecy - a child will be born, the Savior of the world. Direct our thoughts and and guide us each day as we live together. Let us live together in harmony as brothers.
Bless our parents, relatives, and friends at home. Heal those that are sick, and comfort those who are worried and broken hearted because of us, although we are seperated in body, may we be united in spirit in celebrating this Thy Son's birthday.

(continued)

The Unseen Hand

We thank thee oh Father for thou son who was born on this day two thousand years ago, fulfilling the prophesy a child will be born, the savior of the world. Direct our thoughts and guide us each day as we live together.

Let us live in harmony as brothers. Bless our parents, relatives, and friends at home.

"Heal those that are sick and comfort those who are worried and brokenhearted because of us. Although we are separated in body, may we be united in spirit in celebrating this, thou son's birthday.

"Bless both allied and enemy forces on the battlefield, heal the wounded and comfort those who are fighting for a purpose which they think is right before God and man.

"We thank thee for the food which has been provided for us as well as all of the necessities.

"We thank thee for our health and our lives for many are not alive to return home when this conflict is over.

"Bless us as we

face a new year. May our greatest desire be to return home as better Americans and may the word of our mouth and the meditations of our hearts be acceptable in the sight of our Lord and redeemer. Amen."

This was a beautiful prayer from one that was horribly beaten by his enemies. He had so much to forgive and he did.

Chapter 14: Red Cross Telegram

I never received any mail from home the entire time of my confinement. I did receive one wonderful Red Cross cablegram, though, and this one meant the world to me. Had it not been delivered at the time that it was, I would never have received it. I would have never heard the wonderful news about my daughter's birth until later. We left this camp just five days after I had received the cablegram. It would not have been delivered to me while on the march.

The last day of January, early in the morning, the door was opened, and a guard came into the room. Several of us were sitting around the stove trying to stay warm. The guard asked for Sergeant Moore. I saw the cablegram in his hand, and I knew it was news from home. The guard said something that nearly caused me to faint. He said, "Sergeant Moore I have some bad news for you." My buddies said my face turned white. He said, "You have a baby girl." Then he grinned and handed me the cablegram. I almost passed out. The cablegram read: Eight pound baby girl born September 16th, very image of you, love Nell.

The unseen hand...

I still have that cablegram that thrilled me so that day. It helped me to bear the burdens and the heartaches that I faced.

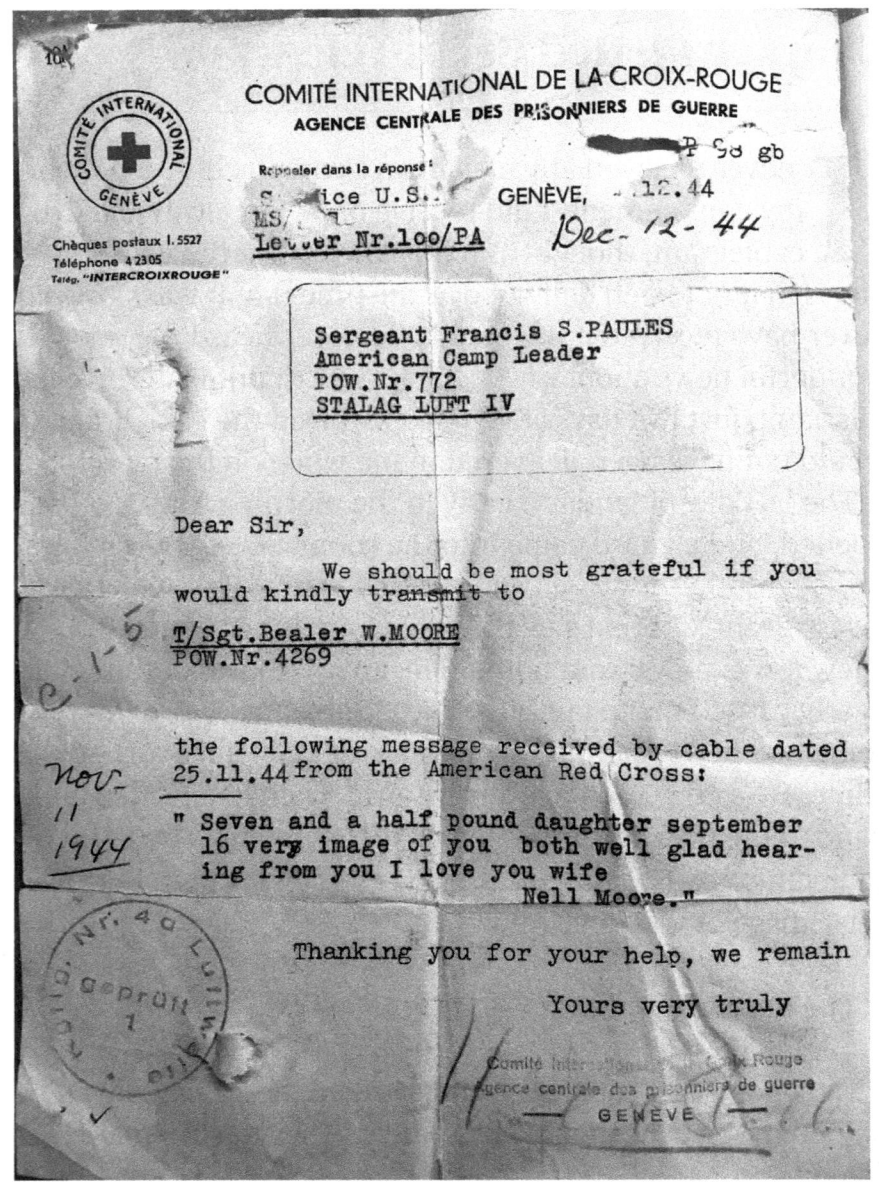

The cablegram announcing Bealer Gwen Moore's birth. Received Jan, 1945.

We knew our time at this camp was about over. We heard the news reports each day that the Russians were closing in on a drive to cut that part of Poland off, and we knew the Germans didn't want the Russians to liberate us. They needed us for bargaining purposes with the allies. We didn't know what kind of transportation they would use to carry us away from this place, and we were praying they would not use the boxcars as they did when they brought us here. We heard large guns at night and saw a lot of airplanes overhead during the day.

One morning at roll call, our German captain told us through our German-speaking interpreter, a P.O.W. from a German village in Texas, that we would soon be leaving this camp and that we would be walking. He told us that we would have a chance to escape, but it would be a very dangerous thing to leave the group on this march. He said there were places in Germany that were called death locations–if one were caught in those places, he would be immediately shot. They were marked with signs in German, but if you could not read German, you would not be warned.

The day before we left, the large gate was opened and a large road packer, the kind that packed roads, came into the gate and started tearing down the grounds in the compound. This road packer got as far as the mess hall when it fell into the tunnel. They found two tunnels leading out from the mess hall in the center of the compound. The Germans knew we were digging tunnels.

About twelve men would sleep in the mess hall each night. They would dig at night. The twelve men would rotate every night so others could dig. This was a very secret operation and very few prisoners knew about the tunnels.

My left leg was still giving me a lot of trouble, but I could walk on it, and I did everyday. But I didn't expect to have to walk three months across Germany. If I had known about the long march, I probably would say that I would never make it.

We thought life in the camp was Hell, but little did we know what we would soon face on the long march across Germany. Most of us in camp just lived one day at a time, trying to make the best of a terrible situation. By this time, our stomachs were accustomed to what little food we ate and it didn't take much for us to live on. Food was about all we thought about, certainly not women. We were probably living on seven hundred calories a day, not enough to do any kind of work. When you stood up, you had to hold onto something because the blood would rush to your brain and you would feel faint for a few minutes.

The Germans would not let any Air Corps prisoners work. We volunteered to work on farms so we could steal food, but they would not agree to let us out of the compound. We even told them we would sign papers that we would not try to escape if they would let us work on the farms.

We all thought life here in the camp was terrible, but we somehow made it. We didn't think much about the problems that we would soon face.

The Unseen Hand

"Leaving Stalag Luft IV" B.W. Moore

Chapter 15: Death March

We were told on the night of February 5th that we would be leaving this camp in the morning. We didn't have much time to prepare for our walk but didn't have much items to prepare anyway: all I had was a blanket, a good warm overcoat, a good pair of G.I. shoes, a change of long underwear, three pair of good socks, one towel, two bath cloths, one bar of soap, and a toothbrush. No extra food or money to worry about.

They fed us that morning, the usual food. They opened all the Red Cross food parcels and divided the food out to us. Then we left the camp for a walk that would last for three months. We had no idea where we were going or how long it would take us to reach our destination.

That first day on the road, we walked about ten miles without dinner. We had several rest periods. Everyone was happy to be out of that camp, but soon found out that it was a pretty good place to be after all. Men that had been imprisoned for two or three years had a rough time that first day, and I am sure some of them didn't make it. About dusk, late in the afternoon, we came to a large barn. The guards counted about one hundred men to sleep in the barn. The others had to walk on until they found another barn for them. I was separated from Jim, Pop, and Goff. (I never saw Jim or Goff again until we were liberated.) I managed to stay with Rex most of the walk. I saw Pop later during the march and was glad to see him... more about meeting Pop in April...

The first night in that barn was not too unbearable. Some barns were very large and could accommodate two or three hundred men. They locked us in with one guard at the back door and one at the front. Only two prisoners were allowed out at a time to use the latrine. If you had to go and two were already out, you either had to wait your turn or do your business in the straw. A lot of men had diarrhea and couldn't wait.

We walked every day regardless of the weather. Some days it would be snowing or sleeting or raining, very few days were pleasant. We averaged about ten miles a day and often with no food.

I will always remember the camp Chaplain the morning we left camp. He gave us a good sermon that dawn, and he told us to steal everything we could to eat. He reminded us about the story in the Bible where David and his men were outlaws hiding from the army of King Saul. He said they were hungry and went into the Temple and ate the shewbread that only the Priests could eat, but God forgave them for stealing the bread. The Chaplain said that God would forgive us for stealing from the Germans in order to survive.

Rex and I decided we would try to stay together, and we did most of the time. Sometimes the guards would count off enough men to fill one barn, and Rex would have to walk on to another barn or I would have to walk again. Usually, Rex would find us a good place to make our beds in the straw and stay with the blankets, and I would see what I could steal to eat. I could steal better than Rex and most of the time I had success.

The German farms were very large with all kinds of livestock and plenty of vegetables. The cabbage, beets, potatoes, onions, carrots were in long trenches dug in the ground and covered with straw. Sometimes we would find a hen's nest and would eat raw eggs. If it was edible, we ate it. The barns would have milk cows milked by slave laborers, and the laborers would never strip the cows of milk because they knew if we got the chance we would come into the barn and milk them. I could milk because we had cows back home. Some of the P.O.W.s were from the north and probably never saw a cow before and they didn't know what to do. I would milk the cow and give them a cup.

Most all of the farms had pigs, and the farmers would feed the pigs potatoes with buttermilk. They cooked the potatoes in large pots, then pour them into large vats with buttermilk. When a guard was not looking, I would kick the hogs away from the vat and fill my sock with potatoes for the march the next day. The old expression "root hog or die" certainly applied to us.

I am sure the warm milk and the extra potatoes were the food that helped Rex and myself to stay alive and able to walk everyday.

Rex and I would share our potatoes on the walk with men who had nothing to eat. We just couldn't bring ourselves to eat in front of men who were starving. Rex and I would tie our sock full of potatoes on our belt, and when the guards would stop for lunch break, we also had something to eat.

Sometimes at lunch a guard would peel an onion, and the smell of that onion would drive one crazy. Of all the food I craved, I craved an onion the most. I can't explain why, but the smell of an onion was something wonderful. I think the onion might have had something our bodies needed for strength.

We very quickly learned how to take care of ourselves in order to stay alive. When it was raining or snowing, I would roll up my blanket and tie it around my waist under my overcoat so it would stay dry. We were warm at night although we didn't have any fire in the barn, but we had plenty of fresh straw to bury down in and stay warm.

Men suffered from blisters on their feet and we had no way to prevent this. No Band-Aids to cover the sores. My G.I. shoes were in good shape, but my feet were sometimes wet from walking in the snow, yet as long as we walked, they would stay warm.

Body lice were another problem. The straw in the barns had lice so it was impossible to destroy them. Most of us had sores from scratching at night.

Everyone suffered from diarrhea.

Our German captain rode in a covered wagon pulled by two oxen. He had a German soldier who would drive the oxen and would feed and take care of them. Every morning this guard

"Pre Flight Charlie" B.W. Moore

would preflight the oxen. He would open their mouths to examine their tongues, and he would feel their ears. Then he'd lift up their tails, though I don't know why he did this. We called him "preflight Charlie." When it was snowing or raining, the captain would ride inside in comfort.

On the march we seldom went through a town. When we did, we were not allowed to walk on the sidewalk. We were treated like dogs. Sometimes a prisoner would have an attack of diarrhea and have to use the street as a toilet. It was very embarrassing when this happened, for civilians would be on the streets, yet it couldn't be helped. Thank God we didn't have to go through many towns. We were in groups of three or four hundred men with three or four guards. We could have escaped any time we wanted but knew it was better to stay with the group. We had already been warned about the danger if we tried to escape. Almost every important crossroad would have a German civilian with a rifle who stood guard.

Everyone did their best to help their buddies. The prisoners that had been in prison for two or three years suffered the most because of their already weak condition. The situation became so bad that the Germans had to bring in wagons to haul the men that couldn't keep up. Some were so weak that they were left by the side of the road. I don't know what happened to them. There were men so weak that they couldn't keep up, and a guard would have to stay with them. This would make the guards mad because the other guards would arrive at the barn and would find a good place to sleep in the house. The ones that had to stay behind sometimes had to sleep in the barn with us.

Chapter 16: Experiences on the March

Life on the march was entirely different from life behind barbed wire. We felt as if we had more freedom. I think what made this possible was that the guards knew we would not try to escape.

The German guards that had to walk with us were in the same sorry condition. They were men that had been in combat, and most were wounded, unfit for combat duty. Most were old men. We would carry their guns for them on the march.

Some would share their meager food with us. Always away from the other guards... they never trusted their comrades. They were issued a loaf of black bread and a bottle of schnapps, some canned pâté, a small can of butter, and a small can of jam.

They knew that the war was coming to an end. They knew they were losing the war. So they became almost friendly nearing the end of the march.

February was a very cold month; in fact, this winter was on record of being the coldest in many years. The first day out of the camp, there was about one foot of snow on the ground. As far as the eye could see, there were prisoners walking four abreast with very few guards. I can't recall many exact dates on this march, yet some I will never forget, such as February fourteenth, Valentine's Day.

In this part of Poland, we didn't see many large roads, and the roads that we did see were crowded with civilians and soldiers. The civilians tried to escape the Russians that drove into the region around the Baltic.

The German soldiers were either going to the front to fight or coming back from the front wounded. It was impossible for the Germans to keep us from seeing their wounded. We were very near the front lines. What we did see was something that surprised all of us, and I am sure the Germans didn't want us to witness this, but couldn't help it. The Red Cross trucks would pass us covered with canvasses. In those trucks going to the front lines were German soldiers going there to fight under the protection of the Red Cross.

We could hear the large guns from the front everyday. We watched a lot of airplanes strafing and bombing.

After walking eleven days, we reached the city of Stettin near a large body of water. The Germans had boats that ferried P.O.W.s across the lake. These boats were very small, like a tugboat, and couldn't carry many men at one time. So, we had to wait a long time. Finally, we were loaded on the boat for the trip across. We were on the lake for about two hours; this was around noon. We reached the shore across the lake and stayed in a large field. No barn to sleep in this night. About four in the afternoon it began to sleet and snow.

We gathered wood to build a large fire which helped us to stay warm and bear the weather but there were so many men that we couldn't gather around the fire for too long. Others had to get warm, so we rotated, taking turns around the fire. We had to keep moving our feet to keep them from freezing.

The German captain finally arrived along with his covered wagon. Once he stepped into the comfort of his wagon, the four of us decided that we could crawl under it to escape the freezing rain and snow. We spread one blanket on the ground and used the other three to cover ourselves. This was one miserable night, but we made it.

After crossing this large lake, we were on German soil. We had no idea of where we were going or how long it would take us to get there, but why worry about how long it would take when the main worry was how to stay alive to make it through each day?

Often, we were on the road with large groups of civilians and German soldiers. A lot of the civilians were Gypsies. The Germans hated these people because they would block traffic with their large covered wagons. These people seemed happy and not at all concerned about the war. They looked healthy as if they had plenty to eat. This probably was their way of life, and the war around them didn't make much difference to them. What surprised me most of all was the fact that there were so many of them. I wondered where they all came from and where they were going.

Most of the German civilians on the road were in terrible condition. They were walking and carrying their possessions in suitcases or in cloth bags on their back. The children were the ones that suffered most; they were hungry and poorly clothed for this terrible weather. I don't know where these people slept, I am sure they had to stay outside a lot of nights because we would see them walk past as we went into the barns for the night.

In this part of Germany there were very little towns or villages. Mostly wooded sections with few buildings of any kind to shelter people. We never had to spend the night outside except for that night of February 14th.

Things happened on this long march that if I should write about, I am sure very few people would believe it. Some were horrible and some were funny. I had rather remember the funny ones other than the horrible ones, but you learn very quickly that unpleasant things will happen, and you must be ready to accept whatever falls your way.

One Sunday when we didn't have to walk, the German farmer, in whose barn we were staying, told us that he would feed us all the potatoes we could eat if we would leave his chickens alone, and not to kill any or eat the eggs. Evidently, he was a government farmer because all of his chickens had numbered leg bands. He had to account for each chicken on his farm.

He left early that morning with his family, and locked the henhouse door before leaving, but he failed to lock the small door that let the chickens out. After all the chickens came out of the henhouse, I closed the small door so the chickens couldn't get inside to lay their eggs. They had to lie in the barn, so we got plenty of eggs that day. I have no idea how many chickens were killed. Very few came out of that barn once they went inside. One Yankee came up to me holding the entrails of a chicken and asked me what part was the liver. Another Yankee followed a chicken around for several hours after it had laid an egg, expecting it to lay another one.

Rex and I were boiling some eggs in a can when one Yank, very excited, told us about finding a bunch of eggs in a nest, with a glass inside the nest. Rex and I knew what he had found, and we congratulated him on his find and decided not to tell him about the eggs. He asked us if we would let him use the fire to boil his eggs and we said okay.

We were anxious to see his reaction when he cooked the eggs to find biddies inside. After they had boiled for a while, he took one out and cracked it and found a biddy. He threw it down and tried again, the same thing happened. Then he peeled another one and found the same thing, but this time he didn't throw it away. He said, "what the Hell, the Chinese eat eggs this way and it don't kill them," and he ate every one of them eggs. Rex and I had to leave, although we weren't surprised that he ate them.

The German farmer came home late in the day and counted his chickens. He almost went nuts when he found so many of his chickens missing. He begged us for the tags so he could report what happened. We found a few of the tags but wouldn't turn them in for fear of punishment. When we left the next morning, we left the tags where he could find them. He might have been shot after we left, but starving men didn't give a damn what happened. We were only concerned about food and how we found it didn't matter to us.

Another incident that happened to us, one when the P.O.W. didn't get off so lucky: the guards told us when we arrived at this barn that the farmer told them he would give us all the potatoes we needed if we would leave his seed potatoes alone. They were in a pile in the middle of the barn. When the farmer and the guard left the barn, men started filling up their pockets with potatoes. The guard came back into the barn, saw us digging through the pile of seed potatoes, and shot a P.O.W. in the shoulder. He was sent to the hospital; I didn't see anyone else on that pile of potatoes after that.

When a person is hungry and starving, believe me, he will eat everything that is available; even take chances to steal it; sometimes he pays for his mistakes. We were walking with a flight surgeon named Dr. Leslie Caplan. He was Jewish, and the German guards knew he was a Jew and would not give him any medical supplies. This doctor had his hands tied because of this, but it didn't stop him from helping all who were sick. He constantly warned us about what to eat and begged us not to drink any water without boiling it first. This was sometimes impossible because we were not allowed to build fires. Most of the German barns had large stoves in them to cook potatoes for the hogs, so we boiled our water in those fires. Sometimes Dr. Caplan would be notified by the guards that a P.O.W. was sick in another barn down the road. He would ask for volunteers to go with him to help the sick prisoner. I went with him several times at the beginning of the march, but I had to stop because of my leg. If the P.O.W. wasn't able to walk anymore, Dr. Caplan would beg the Germans to take the prisoner to a nearby hospital. That was about all he could do because of his limited supply of medicine. He told us to eat charcoal from the fires in the barn when they cooked the potatoes for the hogs. This would help keep down the diarrhea, and it did help to prevent a lot of this problem that everyone suffered from on the march.

One evening after a long walk, Rex had found us a good place in the barn to sleep. Dr. Caplan found me and asked me to go with him to a barn about three miles down the road. A guard told him that a P.O.W. was sick and needed help. We found the barn and the P.O.W. The doctor examined the sick soldier and asked him what he had eaten that day. He told the doctor he had eaten some raw wheat that he found. The doctor told him that he probably had appendicitis and that he would try to get him to a hospital. He asked the guards there to take the P.O.W. to the nearest hospital. After a lot of argument, the guards said they would take him. We don't know what happened to the sick P.O.W., if he made it or not. This was all the doctor could do for him.

Dr. Caplan went the full line of duty and more in trying to help all he could on the march. He was never too tired to go the extra mile and often he would have to walk another four or five miles to a barn where some sick prisoners were, in order to help them as much as he could. He was often tired from walking all day and often at wits end trying to help someone without any medical supplies. He was the most patient man and the most dedicated man I have ever known. When asked by the Army Intelligent Officers after I was liberated if there was anyone who was outstanding on the march who deserved recognition, I told them about Dr. Caplan[3] and that he should receive the highest award they could give anyone. He deserved every medal they could give. I don't know if he received any recognition or not when he returned home, but I hope he did, for he deserved it.

We were always near the front line of battle. One night in our barn, we heard this plane diving and knew it was not a German plane because their engines made a different sound. We heard a loud explosion that shook the barn; it was so close. Shells exploded and bullets whizzed by overhead. We knew we were very close—about two hundred yards away.

The next morning as we left the barn, we had to pass the spot where the truck exploded. There was no way the Germans could bypass this wreck, so we went by this place on the road. We saw two trucks, or parts of two or three trucks, on the road. Evidently, they were hauling shells to the front at night, but these didn't make it. I don't know how many men were killed, but the American pilot sure did his job. The Germans removed the bodies but missed a boot with a leg still in it.

In March there was so much air activity—strafing and bombing by allied planes—that it was dangerous to be on the road walking. The Germans told us that they had received information that our Air Corps had warned them they would strafe anything moving on the roads. The German guards told

---

[3] Dr. Leslie Caplan, "the Death March Medic," continued his service to veterans until his death on August 4, 1969. He worked part-time as a consultant in psychology for the V.A. Hospital in Minneapolis. He was an Associate Clinical Professor of Psychology at the U of Minnesota Col of Medicine. Senator Mark Dayton (Minnesota 2001-2007) nominated Dr. Caplan for the Congressional Medal of Honor.
See Appendix C for Dr. Caplan's testimony.

us to never hit the ditches but to stand and wave our arms so the strafing pilots could see us, and they would know we were prisoners. This might have helped, but at the first sight of a strafing plane, the Germans would put on their helmets and dive for the ditch and we would all do the same. Then, strafing would take place. We were strafed four or five times with a lot of men killed or wounded.

The march was not all horrible. There were times we would have a good laugh. One day we were taking a break beside a small stream with a wooden bridge with wooden rails. Three young German guards with their packs on their backs were leaning against the bridge when the rail broke, and all I saw were the heels of the soldiers going over into the water. Everyone saw what happened but had to hold their sides to keep from laughing. They were soaking wet and mad as Hell. That water was cold as ice around the edge of the stream.

One day after walking, we stayed at a large barn. It was a sunny day and about fifty of us were outside sitting in the sun along the side of a barn. We were very close together to keep warm. A German guard walked with his rifle in front of us. He was about our age, young enough that we knew to keep silent and not cause any trouble. One P.O.W. from Brooklyn, New York, said loud enough for the guard to hear him, "Look at that son of a bitch. He's carrying a Czechoslovakia rifle and he's wearing part infantry pants and a Luftwaffe uniform. They are so damn near beat they don't have sense enough to know they are finished. Why don't they surrender?"

The German guard heard his remarks and threw a shell in the chamber of his rifle and stuck it in the belly of the P.O.W. and said to him, "Say another word and I'll blow your guts out." The P.O.W.? He started sweating and we all slid away from him and left him alone. We didn't even know this German soldier could speak English because he never did before.

The German soldier told us later, when we were away from the other guards, that he was from Brooklyn. He had visited his father in Germany in 1939. The Germans would not let him return home and made him join the army. He later became a good friend and helped us when he was alone away from the other guards. He shared what little food he had with us when he could and would tell us the news about the war. He encouraged us to hold out because the war would soon be over, and we could all go home.

A lot of the large farms where we stayed had locked buildings. We often wondered what they contained. One day, we were at this type of barn with steps, and under the steps was a locked door. This young guard stood in front of the barn and asked us if anyone could pick a lock. We knew that some one in our bunch could. He told us that there was food in the basement because this was a Government storehouse. But he warned us that anyone caught in that basement would be shot. He said that he had an hour left until another guard replaced him.

We knew how to distract guards by offering them cigarettes. Some P.O.W.s had cigarettes from home, and they would walk up to a guard and offer him a smoke. Most of them would accept American cigarettes. While they were talking, we would steal food; sometimes it worked and sometimes it didn't. This time, it did.

We found a P.O.W. that could open a safe if it needed opening. The lock was no problem. Two of us would go under the steps, go into the basement and fill our shirts and pockets with canned food. We knew that meant danger, but we found food that some of us had not eaten for a long time: apples, canned beef, cheese, carrots, onions, all kinds of canned foods were in that basement.

We really made a run on that storage room until an officer drove up in front of the building and caught two men in the basement. He told us that if we would bring back all that was taken, these two men would not be shot. A lot of the food was returned, but some of it had been eaten. He then asked if we would return the cans. The empty cans. He would release the two men if he could account for the cans of food. No one would voluntarily give up the cans for fear of being shot. Finally, the German officer slapped the two men and knocked them down and kicked them several times. Then he let them go. They got off light. I believe he would have shot them if the war weren't so close to being over.

One afternoon when we had finished walking for the day and had found a good place in the barn to sleep, I felt the call to use the bathroom. Usually the toilet was simply out in back of the barn. This barn had a lot of scrub trees around it, and we were using the trees for a place to relieve ourselves. When three or four or five hundred men, walking in a group each day, there are problems that happened to us that might seem terrible to some, but remember, we had to make do with whatever we had. For example, there was no toilet paper. I carried a sock that I used for this purpose, washing it each time after I used it. And no toilets for us to use so we had to go outside.

I was outside in the trees with about thirty other prisoners doing number two when all Hell broke loose. We saw a B-17 bomber falling about half a mile away, and there were three or four ME-109s - German planes shooting at it as it was falling. Shells exploded all around us, and bullets went through the trees and hit the ground. There was a hog pen behind the barn, and some of the hogs were hit and they were squealing. All of us dove to the ground and tried to get as flat as we could.

I heard someone laughing like mad, and I looked up and saw a German guard with his back against a tree. When everything quieted down, I stood up and was covered with human waste - all over my clothes. This really made him crack-up when he saw all this mess on my clothes. When I was able to talk, I asked him how he could remain so calm when the shells and bullets were going off around him. He told me that he had just come from the Russian front and this was child's play to him.

The next morning as we came from the barn, we looked up and saw a German officer hanging from the hay loft in the barn. He committed suicide when told to report to the Russian front lines.

We could tell when a German guard was saying goodbye, leaving for the front, after they had become well enough to fight again. If they were being sent to the Russian lines to fight, or if they had orders to report to the allied front, you could tell which lines they were going to. If it was the Russian front, they would hug their friends and almost cry. They wanted no part of the Russian lines because they knew they would probably never make it back or if they did, they would have some part of their body missing. They knew from firsthand experience how the Russians fought and how brutal they could be. These soldiers that fought on the Russian front were very bitter towards us, never friendly or kind.

Near the end of the march we would sometimes have fresh meat to eat. One day in March, the German captain asked us if we had someone who could dress out a cow. We found several P.O.W.s that had worked in butcher shops before the war, or they had been raised on farms, and knew all about butchering hogs and cows. J.L Byrum, from Elizabeth City, North Carolina, was located in the group. He was also in my room in camp. He knew how to dress and cut up the cow, and we had some beef stew that night for supper. The captain let us build a fire to cook the meat. The cow had been killed in a strafing raid. Our pilots would shoot at anything on the ground, even cows. They probably thought the Germans would let us eat the cows, so they strafed them. The farmers would lock the cows in the barns during the day and let them out at night to graze in order to keep them from being strafed. On the march we would often see cows and horses in the fields that had been killed by strafing. Their bodies would be in another field –while walking on the road they had no way of getting food to us.

The civilians at the barns were sometimes friendly and had compassion for us. Often the slave laborers working on the farms would help us if they could. I will never forget the kind slave woman from Holland that I think might have saved my life. I had a terrible cold and was almost ready to give up. I was so weak that I could hardly walk, even with a crutch made from a shovel handle. She noticed how sick I was and went into the house and brought out a hot bowl of potato soup with onions. I have never tasted anything as good as that soup. One would think that after eating potatoes everyday that I would have turned my nose up at this bowl of soup, but all the potatoes we ate were without any salt or butter. Just plain potatoes, no seasonings, not even salt. This kind lady told me as best as she could that she was brought from Holland when the Germans captured that country, and they made her cook for them on the farm. She also told me that two hundred American officers were burned to death in a barn near this place. They had accidentally set fire to the hay inside the barn and the Germans would not let them out. Often men in our group, in a barn at night would strike a match, never realizing how dangerous this could be because of the hay in the barn. This didn't happen too often, we didn't have many matches, but when it did happen, men would raise Hell at the one responsible.

Walking across Germany and seeing firsthand the way the Germans lived and how they managed to make the best out of a bad situation fascinated me. Often, we would see a family all bundled up riding in a sleigh pulled by a beautiful horse through the snow. It would remind me of a Currier and Ives painting. Life here reminded me of reading about life in our country during the 19th century. Sometimes we would see a Volkswagen car, a Beetle with a bundle of wood on top and a large boiler in the rear of the car with a fire going in the boiler. This was their fuel. Sometimes they'd just put wood in the boiler.

The barns were built onto the house and were always very clean inside, nothing smelled like hog pens. Every few miles we could come to a small group of houses and barns surrounded by large fields that were clean with no rocks in them. One thing that impressed me most was the beautiful forest that we walked through. The ground under the trees was absolutely free of limbs and no brush. The farmers would gather each twig up and tie them into bundles and stack them near the house.

Another thing that we saw and couldn't understand was the large herds of deer and how small they were. They were no larger than dogs, and we would often see large bunches of them together. We found out that the Germans had orders from Hitler not to kill anything. So, they interbred and became small.

The Germans that lived and worked on the farms for the most part were very fortunate to be on the farms and not in the cities. They had food and everything to make life bearable. They were dressed very well and looked well-fed, but they were never happy. Even the young children we saw on the farms never laughed. They saw all the suffering and misery of the wounded soldiers coming from the front lines.

It seemed to me that all through this country there was the smell of death. It was everywhere, there was no escaping it. Death was in the air and on the ground. It was impossible for anyone to be happy living with death all around, and it could happen at any time.

Another strange thing to me was how dark it was at night. You never saw a light except from the flashes of a city being bombed or from the large guns and exploding shells.

I never tried to keep up with the days; one day was just the same as another. I didn't know the month or the day but the first day of April was different. The weather was about the same; some days were sunny and pleasant. We still had to walk every day, and didn't know where we were going. The guards were not so hateful or mean now as they were at the beginning of the march. I guess they knew that the war was about over. Every day we saw our planes flying overhead; the fighters flying escort with the bombers. It was sad to see the bombers going overhead knowing they would return to a warm bed with plenty of good food.

We were near the town of Hanover. Near this town was a Russian prison called Falling-hostel. The Germans put us in a large compound that was empty and warned us not to go over into the Russian compound because they were dying with Typhus. This was a horrible place, one that I will never forget. The Russians did not have Red Cross support, and they were starving and dying.

Each morning the Germans would bring in a wagon and would carry out Russian bodies stacked like wood. We were told that we would be here for five days because of the air activity around this place. We saw planes every day.

About the second day in this camp, I was going to the toilet and was hardly able to walk with my crutch when I passed a P.O.W. that looked very familiar to me after he passed me. I turned around and said, "James?" He stopped and turned around and looked at me, and I knew it was James Pentecost, from home. Words can't describe the joy at this meeting, although we both hoped that we would never meet under these conditions. But we also knew it might happen for we both were going into combat on heavy bombers. James and I shared a tent at this horrible camp. He told me that he and his friend were going to crawl under the outdoor toilet and stay there until they were liberated. We knew the war was almost over because of the planes we saw each day and we could hear the small guns' fire getting closer each day. He pleaded with me to stay with him, but I told him it was too risky and I had come this far and didn't want to risk getting killed by staying behind.

After five days here, the Germans called us out early one morning for the march. I didn't see James and I knew where he and his friend were hiding. *James and his friend were liberated the next day and were sent home, arriving before I was even liberated. He told some friends that he had met me, and I was in terrible condition and he didn't think that I would make it. Somehow this word got back to Nell and my family. It must have been Hell for them to receive that rumor.*

That morning we were lined up for the march, and I saw a P.O.W. stick his foot under a heavy load of sugar beets on a wagon. The heavy load broke his foot, and he was sent to a nearby hospital. *He was also liberated the next day. I walked on for another month.*

I celebrated my birthday, April 15th, with some cold potatoes but was thankful to be alive. That day I was walking past a German guard, and I was singing "It's a long way to Tipperary," when a German guard heard me and made the remark, "but you're not going there." Then he told me that our President was dead. We didn't believe him, but later on we were told it was true.

The next day we were sitting outside alongside a barn in the warm sunshine when something that looked like a plane came roaring by very near the ground. It virtually scared the Hell out of us. It was a German jet. The noise sounded like thunder.

(This is what I saw on a mission to Schweinfurt on July 19th, that I reported in my diary. We were never attacked by jets on our missions and really didn't know anything about this German aircraft.)

Behind the barbed wire at Stalag Luft IV, we never saw our planes we could only hear them. We never saw them because the Germans would rush us inside the barracks and shut the blinds over the windows. We often heard the bombs explode. But on the march, we would look up and see contrails from the bomber formations.

May the second is a day I will never forget. We had just left the barn after preflight Charlie had gone through his ritual, checking out the oxen and had walked about a mile from the barn when our formation was stopped. It was so foggy you couldn't see over one hundred yards ahead. A German dispatcher came by us on a motorcycle in an awful hurry, and the captain tried to flag him down, but he flew by and didn't stop. Evidently, he was trying to get through, but he didn't make it. Up ahead we heard machine gun fire, and he returned to us; he appeared to be shaken up. He stopped this time and told the captain what happened.

We soon found out why he came back. We heard something coming toward us through the fog and suddenly a large tank appeared. The tank stopped in front of the wagon and the lid opened, then a head came out of the tank and yelled to us, "Take their guns and blow their bloody guts out!" It was a tank from the British 2nd Army. We knew it was all over for us; the long march was finally over for us.

We were liberated.

The Unseen Hand

"Liberation Day: May 2nd, 1945" B.W. Moore

Chapter 17: Liberation

You can't imagine the feeling of being free again. Four to five hundred men shouting and laughing, crying and hugging one another. Words cannot describe this scene. We were so happy to be free that everyone forgot how horribly the Germans had treated us. I never saw anyone beat the guards, although I did see the slave laborers beating the farmers.

I had a friend from Texas, and he often told me that he was going to make that captain give him his boots if we were ever liberated. I would always laugh when he told me he was going to have those beautiful boots. He kept his word. He made the captain give him his boots and he immediately put them on his feet. *The next time I saw him was in the hospital at camp Lucky Strike in France. His feet were in terrible condition, and he was cursing the captain. He had the worst case of athlete's feet and was sent to the hospital.*

The tank commander told us there was a small village about five miles down the road. He told us to go there for the night. He said that if we encountered any Germans that would not let us have their houses, to come back for him, and he would force them out. He also told us that we would have to walk about ten miles to a town where they had transportation for us. He said to take anything that we could ride on. If we had trouble, to come back for him. The war was still going on and they didn't have transportation for us.

We had gone about two miles down the road when bullets whizzed by our heads. They came from a patch of woods about two hundred yards away. We all hit the ditch, and someone crawled back to the tank. The tank came back, and fired one round into the wooded area, and about twenty-five SS troopers came out with their hands over their heads. We finally reached the houses in the village about four o'clock in the afternoon.

The first night in this house was one I will never forget. We had a ball. This was a beautiful house with about six bedrooms. Beside the front door was a hole about the size of a gallon bucket, a shell hole. You could look through the hole all the way through the house; the shell went through and didn't explode. In the kitchen was a bucket of potatoes, about half were peeled, and not even turned brown. The occupants of this house must have heard the British were coming and left in a hurry. They just picked up their clothes from the dresser drawers and fled.

This house was immaculate. Even the barn built onto the house was spotless, no smell from the cows. One bedroom had a large oil portrait of Hitler, and I am sure it would have been a valuable souvenir, but someone had cut a slice down the middle of it. I found a chest full of silverware, about an eight-place setting that sparkled, but after walking across Germany, and still having to walk another ten miles, I passed up this collection.

I also found a beautiful shotgun, but I broke the stock around a tree and left it. The only thing I picked up was a straight razor to shave with, and it was a good razor. It's about the only souvenir that I brought home with me. I was barely able to walk, and didn't need anything heavy to carry.

This house had a cellar stocked with all kinds of food and wine. We had been warned by Dr. Caplan not to eat anything when we were liberated, and not to drink any wine or beer. These words of warning went in one ear and out the other for most prisoners. I found some oatmeal, and I went into the barn, and milked a cow for my oatmeal. All through the house P.O.W.s were looking for something to eat, and they found a lot of food in the cellar. They were opening cans of meat, and eating everything in sight. Also drinking wine and beer.

In every bedroom of the house, men were in bed with a table pulled up filled with wine and beer bottles. I looked in one room and laughed so hard it hurt. Five P.O.W.s were in one bed with a table full of wine and each had a white night cap on and in pajamas and the wine had spilled down the pajamas looking like blood. It was all over the sheets, but they were having a ball and didn't give a damn about anything. I am sure they paid for this fling the next day on the road.

We had a long walk the next day, and I saw men so sick they couldn't even walk; most were passing blood, and most everyone had a bad case of diarrhea; some were vomiting.

We walked about five miles and came to a small town. Someone had opened a vault in the bank and money was all over the street. People were filling their pockets with the paper money. I picked up four bills thinking it was no good, I just wanted some to take home as a souvenir.

When we reached the port to get on the ship for home, I found out that money printed before 1939 was good, but I only had a few bills that were printed with that date.

The British met us on the road with a truckload of pistols that they dumped on the ground and told us to help ourselves to them. I picked up two not knowing if I could bring them home (so I eventually sold them to a sailor on the return trip).

On the road that day I saw every kind of vehicle that would move, carrying men. I even saw a tractor with a wagon behind it loaded down with men, and they were having a good time. We had walked about three hundred miles, and they were enjoying a ride for a change.

There was even this one joker from Texas who rode a horse. He claimed that he was taking the horse back to Austin.

Meeting us on the road were about four or five thousand German soldiers. They were going to a P.O.W. camp and had very few British soldiers walking with them.

We stopped a small German car with a German captain and his wife inside. He didn't want to give us the car, but we asked a British soldier to make him get out of the car. He grabbed the officer by the collar and pulled him out of the car. We finally had some transportation, but not for long.

About five miles down the road we came to a river that had a bridge, but the bridge was bombed, and we couldn't cross. Men were being ferried across the river on small boats.

In a large field I saw every kind of vehicle parked. That was as far as we could ride. The water was so cold that no one could swim across. We had to wait our turn on the boats.

The Texan finally made it to the river, and we wondered how he was going to get his horse across. We didn't have long to wonder what he would do. He stripped down to his long johns, tied his clothes to the saddle horn and swam the river with his horse.

I met him four months later in Texas and asked him if he made it with his horse, and he told me that the only trouble he had with the horse was that he had to have him vaccinated. They let him bring the horse back on the boat and he shipped the horse home by train.

No one would believe the souvenirs I saw on the ship coming home. Men had all kinds of guns, oil paintings–even one guy had an accordion. I wanted a camera. The British told us there was a camera factory near by and to help ourselves to the cameras, but I was too tired to walk over to the factory. Some men went and brought back beautiful cameras. I just wanted to get home in one piece and didn't want to take any risks, the war was still going on and we were still in Germany.

We finally reached a town where the Americans met us with large trucks that carried us to a railroad station. From there we went to Brussels, Belgium. At Brussels we received our first delousing.

You can't imagine how good that first hot shower felt to us. We take so much for granted in this country. We didn't want to leave that hot water.

After the shower we went into a room, and they covered us with white powder. Then they gave us all new clothes. I went through five delousing sessions before getting on the train for France.

We went through Holland on train and finally arrived at Camp Lucky Strike in France. When we arrived at this camp, the head cook was going to prepare us a meal fixed for a king, but a doctor chewed him out telling him he would have killed about half of us, feeding us that meal.

We were fed nothing but eggnog. They had barrels and barrels of eggnog and that is all they would allow us to eat or drink.

I met John Honeycutt here at this camp. I didn't know that the Germans had captured him. The last time I saw him was in high school. We played football together.

One night at this camp, John and I decided we were going to find something to eat. We were hungry and the eggnog was getting old. We saw a soldier guarding a large tent. We went up to him and explained to him that we were ex-P.O.W.s and that we were hungry. He asked us where we lived in the States, and we told him we were from Roxboro, North Carolina, and he said he was from Roxboro, too. He went under the tent and brought out a large can of peaches and a can of milk. We really enjoyed those peaches and milk but what was so surprising to us was this soldier was from our hometown.

The next day I went to his tent and gave him a carton of cigarettes. *Several years later at home, I was in a country store one night, Bird's Grocery, where I would often go and shoot the breeze about the war with other veterans when a guy walked in with part of a uniform on. I asked him where he had served during the war, and he told me he spent most of his service in France. I asked him where in France, and he told me Camp Lucky Strike. Then he told me about meeting two guys from Roxboro one night while standing guard at the mess tent. He said they were hungry, and he gave them some peaches. He said he had forgotten their names, and I told him you are looking at one of the men now. I bought him some beer–strange things happen during war.*

John and I stayed together until we reached home. I will never forget the boat trip home. John was seasick the minute we went up that gangplank on the boat. I really felt sorry for him. We were on that ship fourteen days, and he was sick the whole trip. He would get in line at the mess hall but would have to leave. I would bring him his food, but he couldn't keep it down. We were in a storm for three days and this made it worse for him.

I wasn't sick a single day during the terrible storm. I slept out on the deck every night except during those three days of the storm.

I saw men so seasick that they would not have cared if that boat went down during the storm. Some of the men would be hanging over the side vomiting and were told how dangerous it was for them to do that, but they wouldn't pay attention to anyone that tried to help them. They just didn't care what happened.

Sometimes the odor in the hull of that boat was horrible. I would beg John to sleep up on deck with me because of the stench. But he couldn't make it; he was so sick.

We finally reached Newport News, Virginia, and when we got off the boat, we all bowed down and kissed the soil. I am sure a lot of prayers were said that day.

We were allowed to call home with a limit of five minutes. We had to wait our turn in line of about four hundred men waiting to call home. The wait was nothing compared to hearing my wife's voice for the first time in over one year.

We were sent to Camp Patrick Henry, Virginia. This camp was located near a swamp on the coast. I had never heard of this camp before. They had a lot of German P.O.W.s at this facility, and it was strange to be served in the mess hall by these Germans. They were very friendly. These prisoners had it made, and they knew it. Some didn't want to go back home. Quite a difference from the conditions that we had just gone through. But such is war, and I am thankful to have made it home.

We left Camp Patrick Henry by train for Fort Bragg, North Carolina, where we received all of our back pay, including combat pay. That was the most money that I have ever owned at one time.

Nell met me in Raleigh where we spent three days before going home. Her parents kept our baby Gwen while she was with me.

Gwen was about eleven months old at that time, and when I held her in my arms for the first time, I thought she was the most beautiful baby in the world.

At first, she wouldn't have anything to do with me. It was strange, her feeling that way towards me, but I understood why. And it was several days before she became accustomed to me.

Meeting my family and Nell's family was wonderful. A lot of my friends were coming back home, and it was amazing meeting them and sharing our experiences together.

We would all get together at night at Bird's Grocery. We'd sit in the handwoven rockers around that black pot-bellied stove, chewing tobacco, and have a good time exchanging war stories. It was almost too much for me, but I was so grateful to be home.

My church had its annual pot-luck dinner, yet with all that home-cooked food, I still could not eat. But I enjoyed meeting all my friends again.

I received a letter about two weeks after being home from the War Department asking me if I would like to go to Miami Beach for three months with my family to stay in a hotel with all expenses paid. This was a program for all P.O.W.s to recuperate. The letter also told me that I could stay at home and would be paid the money that it would cost the Government for the stay in Miami.

I decided to stay at home the three months. I am sure it would've been a nice vacation, but I was at home and I didn't want to leave.

Afterword

by Mark Moore

Looking back, as his son, I'm frequently reminded of how unusual a dad Bealer was for those times. Unusually attentive. The neighborhood was full of veterans and their families. He must have taught two dozen kids how to swim and dive at our local swimming pool. He spent a great deal of time with my friends and me. He took us fishing, camping, and hunting.

After he put in his time at USPS each day, he would come home to hobbies or spending the afternoon with me. He would take a dozen of us to a field for pick-up games of baseball. He'd be the pitcher and the umpire. If this sounds too ideal, it's because it was.

One of his favorite hobbies was painting. He was quite the accomplished self-taught artist. He must have painted hundreds of pictures in his life, almost all of which he simply gave away.

He could have made a good living as an artist if he had chosen to do so.

I once had a friend who saw a pair of duck decoys he hand-carved and painted. (They're still on my mantle, today.) She asked me if he would carve her a pair. She'd pay him for his efforts. I asked him, and he did. It took him about 40-50 hours to complete the set. I told him that she wanted to pay for them, and wanted to know how much she owed. He said, "Nothing. God gave me this gift, and it's not to make money." So, I delivered the ducks to my friend. When she asked what she owed, and I told her Dad's reply, she told me that she'd priced them, and promptly wrote a check for $500. The following Sunday at lunch, I gave him the check, thinking he would be pleasantly surprised. He wasn't. He was quite angry with me. So, I took the check, gave it to my mother, and she gave it to their church. He was none the wiser. I tell this story only to illustrate just what kind of man my dad was.

My whole life, I remember him teaching Sunday school at our church. He would only miss the occasions due to illness or possibly a fishing trip to the coast.

After retiring in 1976, he and my mother built a house, and moved to Belews Creek, North Carolina. They had about 3 acres of land, where they grew their own food. They had many good years in Belews Creek. There, dad continued teaching Sunday school, and even filled in for the minister when needed. I heard him preach a few times, and he could have easily had a career as a minister if he had chosen to do so.

Mom passed in June of 2001, and dad followed her in June of 2002.

As I mentioned earlier, Bealer was a unique father and man. He was extremely well-liked by everyone. He lived his life as a "true Christian," and by this, I mean that he really tried to live as Christ directed. If someone needed help, he was there. He was never judgmental, always kind and helpful. My wife jokingly tells me that my parents were the biggest reason she had for marrying me. The thing is, I know that she's only half-kidding.

My parents had three children: Bealer Gwen, Cyndi, and me. They also had five grandchildren: Mike, Tracy, Todd, Abbey, and Brian. They were unique grandparents as well. They just knew how to treat us all. It was like a gift.

After my dad passed in 2002, my sister Gwen asked me on several occasions to take our dad's manuscript, journal and sketches, and publish this P.O.W. memoir in his honor. I simply didn't have it in me to take on this endeavor. Fortunately, Todd (Gwen's son) took on this project. Without his work, this book wouldn't have been possible. Todd holds a doctorate in American Literature from UNC-Greensboro. His dissertation focuses on how to ethically respond to representations of trauma that are found in literature. A research topic that was heavily influenced by my dad's experience.

I hope that you've enjoyed his book. I'll always be proud that he was my dad.
- Mark Moore

Appendix A: Red Cross Sketchbook

Editor's note: what follows are additional pages from Bealer Moore's sketchbook that wouldn't fit anywhere in the narrative of the memoir. These images are from the Red Cross book that Bealer carried with him during his time at Stalag Luft IV and the March.

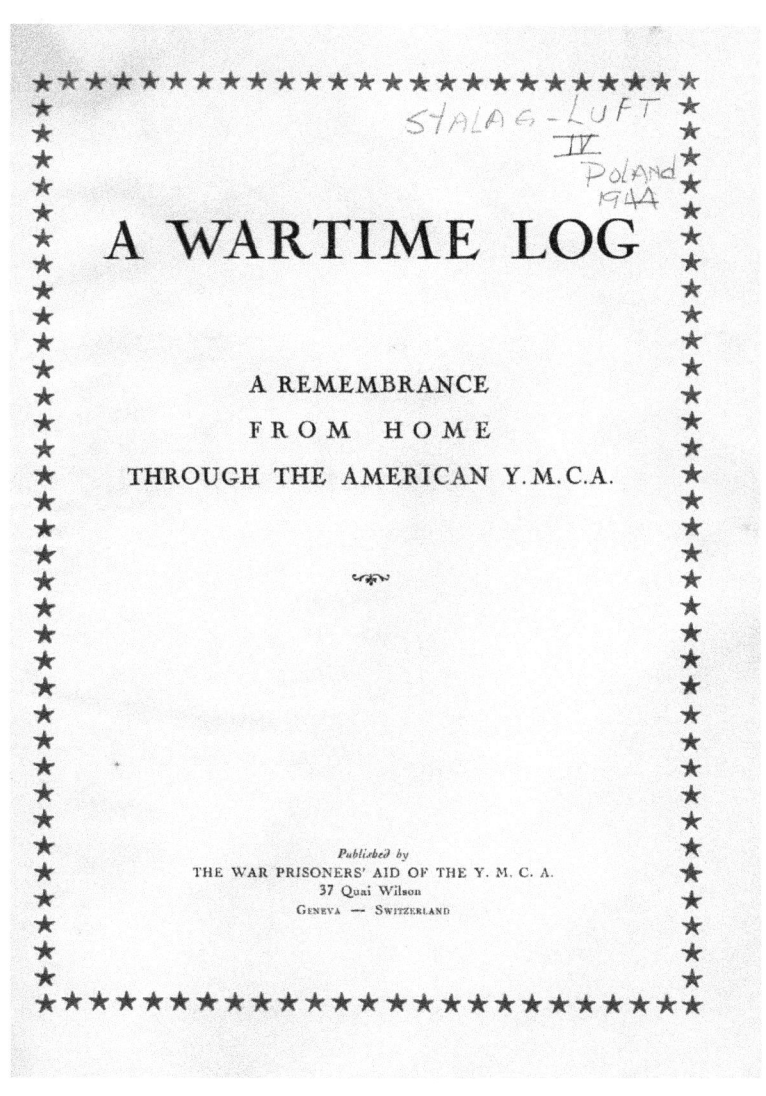

NAVIGATOR

BOMBARDIER

LT. AUGUSTUS CARAS.

LT. EDVARD KONOPACK

16

RADIO

MOE'S OFFICE

WAIST

JAMES RAKOSNIK
WILLIAM NELSON

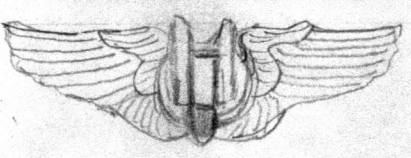

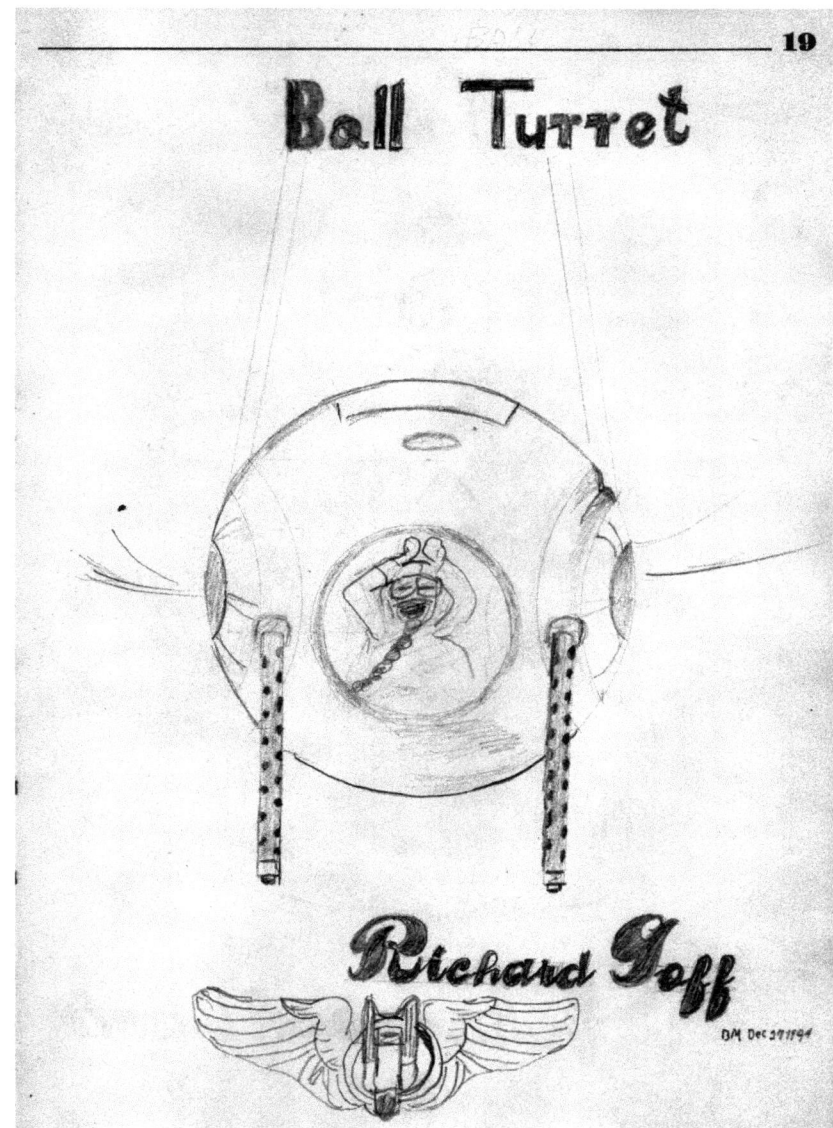

The Unseen Hand

"The Cup"
3-12-1945

A PRISONER'S PRAYER

God my creator and proctor I know that Thou are near me. And so I adore thee Body and Soul and with complete submission to thy will.
Thou hast saved me from death which has overtaken many of my companions And has permitted me to become a Prisoner of war.

'THE' KRIEGIE CREED

I believe in a sort of something somewhere as the theory of Evolution has been proved. I'm not quite sure of a maker of Heaven and Earth. I believe in Jesus Christ one of the greatest men that ever lived. That is of course if he did live, I have no proof of it. If I'm not certain he lived. I can't be certain he died or rose again.

As for his descending into hell and ascending into heaven. That's old fashion and I don't think such places exist.

I believe in the Holy Ghost a vague influence over God but, I've never really understood it. I don't think it necessary to believe in the Catholic Church, Why should I?

I don't know what one means by the Communion of Saints, I don't worry about my sins. I guess that there will be some kind of everlasting Life, but how or what I don't know.

THAT'S WHAT I THINK ?

The Unseen Hand 175

Dec 26 1944
A Kriegie's Dream

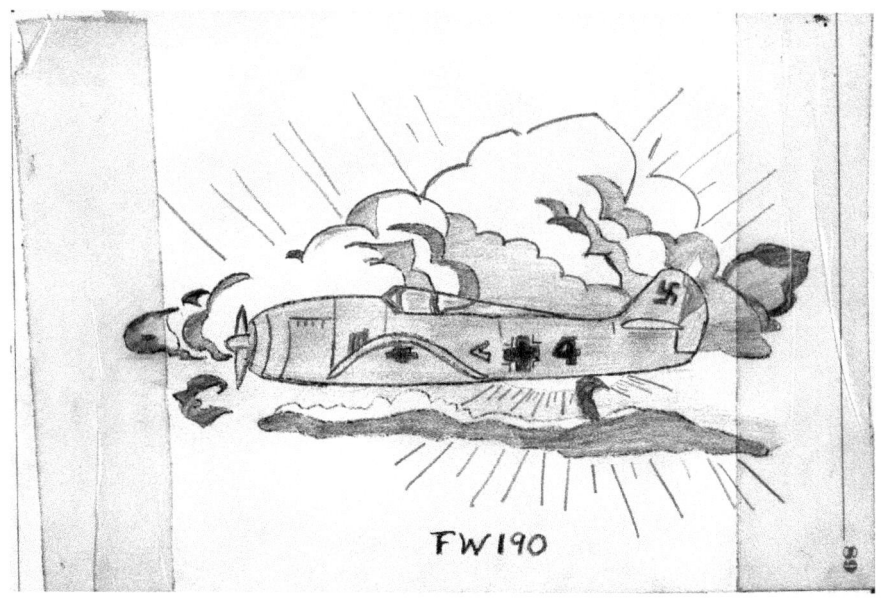

YOU CAN'T BEAT A G.I.

His mother would call him a problem chile,
Then he was drafted and changed his style.
      Now he's what we call a G.I.,
        He's altogether a different guy!
He's fidgety, he's nervous, and afraid of a Gale,
What he needs now is a bucket of Ale.
      His mother still loves him, his girl thinks he's swell.
      But he's a changed man now due to bomb shell.
That's a G.I. some call him "dog face."
You can find him in the most unusual place,
      He's full of ambition, always on the go.
      Even if he is wrecking the show.
He's really handicapped; he can't get Rum?
He gets mischievous, just chewing gum.
      That's a G.I. just full of noise.
      With plenty of ideas, humor and poise.
He never steals but he always will borrow,
But he fails to return it on the morrow.
      Bet that's a G.I., ten to one!
      Tearing the fence down all in fun.
He'll voice his opinions on every damn thing
And when he gets through you'll need an airing.
But what in the "Hell" am I talking about?
I'm a G.I., too, and not a boy-scout.
              John Kostecki, P.o.W.

THE WESTERNER

My fathers sleep on the sunset plains
and each one sleeps alone
Their trails may grow dim to the
    grasses and rains
For I choose to make my own
I lay proud claim to their blood + name
But I lean on no dead kin for praise
    or scorn
For the world began when I was born
and the world is mine to win
They built high towns on old logsills
Where the great slow rivers gleam
But with new live rock from the
    savage hills
I'll build as they only dream.
The smoke scarce dies where the
    trail camp lies
As the rails glint down the pass
The desert springs into fruit + wheat
and I lay the stones of a solid street
over yesterday's untrod grass

I waste no thought upon my neighbors
    births
Nor the way he makes his prayer.
If his game is straight I call him
mate and grant him a white man's
room on earth. If he plays it square
If he cheats, I drop him flat
For old class + rank are all worn out
All clean men are as good as I
and a king is only that.
I dream no dream of a nursemaid
state, that will spoon me out of
my food for the stout heart sings
in the fray with fate.
And the shock + sweat are gone, all
the earthly boon I ask my God
    to share.
So a little daily bread in store
with room to fight the strong
for more, and the weak shall
get their share.

(continued)

108

The sunrise plains are a tender haze, the sunset seas are grey, and the western world is all ablaze.
As the sun wheels swiftly from day to day.
What use to me is the vague "maybe" or the mournful "might have been" for the world began when I was born and the world, it is mine to win

By - Clark.

WHAT WAS HIS NAME

What was his name that lad so young
Who had in silk and strings, his life had hung
Oh yes, it did, if I recall
The day he made that eternal fall

What was his name, that lad so brave
Who fought for his ship, then life to save
There were many fighters, with one desire
To see that fort go down on fire

So in they came, they did their best
There was the flame, he would do the rest
Over the phone, came the pilots shout
O.K. boys, here's where we get out.

"OUT IN THE BLUE"

When you're back home where peace prevails
And begged by all for thrilling tales
Tales of folks you've seen and met
And inclines you'll never forget
Tales of things which soldiers do
And the price they pay in winning them.
Refer to them as "Out of the blue".

The City Throbs With Pulse Of Life

With commerce and industry ever at strife
With hustle and bustle and traffic roar
Far from the distance sound of war

The parks are draped with their floral gowns
And peace prevails in the old town
The Bombers roar and the siren moan.
Are things, thank God, which are quite unknown

But way out here in the distant blue
There's a living hell which men go through
Its day by day, and night by night.
They are locked in the worlds worst fight

As couragesly they stagger and reel
To ward off the menacing nazi heel
To spare all the loved ones they left behind
From the rape and bondage the foe have in Mind

Yet down in the city, if you seek you will find
Men who have chosen to stay home behind
Watching the light on the silvery screen
Sipping their whiskey calm and serene

Reading the paper discussing the news
Laughing and joking and airing their views
Sleeping each night in a cozy warm bed
While their fellow men crash to earth stone dead.

Continued

Out on a mission with target in mind
Jerry will meet you, he loses no time
Reaping the harvest awful and grim
Which Germany long promised to him

The harvest of youth on the threshold of life
All traped in the mow of the titamic struggle
Your husbands your sweethearts, and even
your son.
Gallently fighting and maning their guns
Yet down in the city seek and you will find
Men who have chosen to stay home behind
Where theirs sport each week end in flannel
Pants and a cinema, dinner and mabie a dance!

At while holding you close in uniformed arms
They whisper nice things and tell of your
Charms
They speak of their lore and loyalty to you
As long as it keeps them out of the blue.

Riding our ships in an altitude glide
Death goes around with his arrogant stride
Whispering the name of some one he loves
As fighters scream down from the sky up above

To shower our bombers with muderous aim
On the men they've been sent to cripple and main
Leaving them fall in smoke and flame
To bleed to cry out to die and to choke.
    Continued

Still in the city, if you seek you'll find
Those men who have chosen to stay home behind
Stout hearted fellows with hearts of pure gold.
Gold which is yellow so we are told.

Eager to share in the peace victory brings
Claiming their rights to Life precious things
Proud of the fact they had nothing to lose
Theirs was the choice and thus did they choose

When the battle is over and victory is won.
When the hell and the carnge and gunfire is done
When homeward they march those fortunate few
To pick up the threads of Life they once knew.

How well they will know as they march down
The street
Which echoes to the tramp of their marching
Feet
That the value they placed on their homeland
And you
Was settled and paid for out in the blue

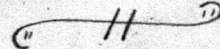

A GUNNERS thoughts

After this war is over, and the boys come home
Again, many are the tales that will be told of
And by the aerial gunner.
In gunnery school the boys got this little poem.

> I wished to be a pilot
> And you alone with me
> But if you all were pilots
> Where would the air force be
> The pilot is just a chauffer
> His job is to fly the plane
> It is we who does the fighting
> Although we don't fame.
>
> It takes guts to be a gunner
> To sit out in the tail
> When the fighters are comming in
> And bullets wail
> So if some must be gunners
> Let us make this bet,
> We will be the best dammed best
> Gunners the enemy ever met.

My Future With Her

It just a year ago
We said so long short and sweet you know
She said she would wait for me
No matter how long the war would be
Soon the time will come for me to go home
And I will be like a king on a throne
I'll always have her by my side
For now she's my own sweet bride

We'll have a house and a little ground
For just the children to run around
I know how happy we will be
Just us four, the wife, two kids and me
These are my future plans you see
That's the way I'd like it to be
Things will run smooth all the time
I'll be happy with her love and she with mine

A Childs Soliloquy

You wont be comming home I guess
To see this pretty yellow dress
You know I kinda thought you would
Cause ive been so awful good

No body ought to be away
I think of Jesus christmas day
I wonder why they have a way
What are Little children For!

My poor mommie cries and cries
But I'm a big girl for my size
And I remember what you said
Bout crying ---- so I don't ... instead

Gee I hope you didn't pain
I hope they kept you from the rain
Of all the men on Land and sea
They had to take you from me

If I could wish upon a star
I bet I'd fly to where you are
But I'm so awful little, --- gee
Nobody pays any mind to me

Thats why I miss you dad
You were the bestest Friend I had
You were the goodest looking man
In all the world from land to Land

Mommie said that you would bring
Me back a doll and every thing
But I know better than what they say
Cause I know why you went away
Continued

And I would rather have you back
And throw away my train and track
My soldiers are all on the floor
I don't play soldier any more

God's Minute
— Something to think about —

I have only just a minute
Only 60 seconds in it
Forced upon me Can't refuse it
Didn't seek it Didn't choose it
But its up to me to use it
Give account if i abuse it
Suffer if i lose it
Just a little tiny minute
But eternity is in it

122

"Bomber's Goal"

They soared across the pale blue sky
A thousand Bombers on high
Over the sea and over the land
To hit the target or be dammed
While far below on the ground
Villagers scatter that heed their sound
Where do they go, the civvies cried
I'll bet I know the braggart sighed
Berlin or Munich yelped another
Kiel or Frankfort, said his brother
Roared the braggart pointing West
I'll bet my shirt they go to Brest
But though they guess a thousand places
And if they guess a thousand objects
None can guess where the "Forts" flew
None were sure but the crew
While in the "Forts" the gunners kept
A vigil watch, for it was life or death
From the guns of two flying machine
Silence reigned on the interphone
Broken only by an oxygen check
Jerry! Jerry! In the Sun

It was the enemy so the fight begun
The gunners sweat, swore and prayed
And fired the guns they oiled that day
Rockets cannons, slugs they all came
Whizzing through the bomber wall
Onward through the bombers did struggle
To reach their target and drop their trouble
Just ahead their quest and crew Flak
Ahead their crew all knew
Far behind the Jerry's left
But on went the bombers to do their best
No 4 began to falter
But through it all our course didn't alter
Now the crew was hard as a rock
Bombs away! Our job was done.

"Janie"

Here you'll find the humorus side of the kriegs
Thoughts. keep your mind clean — Read on
Her name was Janie, she was one of the best
Then came the night I gave her the test
I looked at her with joy and delight
for she was mine for all that night
She looked so pretty so sweet and slim
The night was dark the lights were dim

I was so excited, my heart skipped a beat
For I knew that night I was in for a treat
I'd seen her stripped I'd seen her bare
I'd felt all around her I'd felt everywhere
We started off and she screamed for joy
For this was her very first night with a boy
I got her as high as quick as I could
I handled her well her responce was good

I turned her over then right on her side
Then on her back all ways I tried
It was a great thrill she was the best
In the land. that four engine ship
Of the Bomber Command.

130

A Gunners day

A gunners day is never done up at dawn before
The sun with the roar of engines in our heads
Wishing we could have stayed in bed
Chow at four fried eggs and such wont have time
For much Briefing at five the crew is all their
All anxious to be up in the air see to your chutes
Ammo and guns for all the boys know it not for fun
Jerry will be their up in the blue waiting for someone
Mabie for you take off at six perhaps at six thirty
Hope no one has a gun that is dirty
Form the group at 12000 ft see that formation
It really looks neat put on your oxygen mask
The air is getting thin off to the battle always with
A grin were over the water now test your guns
Enemy coast now comes the fun flak at six flak at
Twelve look out boys there giving us hell here comes
The fighters comming in low mabie their ours dont
Shoot till you know P51's and P38's our escort
Is here they are never late the fighting fools
Each man and his ship there isnt a Jerry they
Couldn't whip the air is cold just 50° below
Turn up the heat so you don't freeze a toe.
A sharp lookout the target is neat we don't want
To meet the enemy here target below plenty of
Flak bombs away now we head back

131

Comming out of the sun enemy ships aim true
We've still got more trips their goes one down
Another one too Our fighters are busy too see none
Get through there are flames in the air as
Another goes down the pilot bails out makes it safe
To the ground then in our tail our own guns start
To roar! theirs blood on your guns you shoot as
Before your ship is hit but stays in the air
You think of your loved ones or whisper a prayer
Smoke from the target leaps into the sky
We'll show these jerrys we know how to fly the fighters
Have left us the ones that were left our fighters got
Some we got the rest we've been up 8 hrs 2 hrs
Too go though were doing 200 it seems very slow
England at last we are informed we think of buddies
Who will never return were over the field the crew
Gives a sigh we've finished another "to do or to die"
Wheels touch the ground with a screech and bump
Our ship brought us back over the hump were tired
And dirty and sore the suns gone down over an hr
Before first clean your guns as good as before
That gun is life his mine or yours a sandwitch
And coffee your chute to turn in down to the
Briefing room drink in your gin two meals
A day and both at night gets on your nerves

132

But we're ready to fight the mess hall is warm in
The cold of the night you sit down and talk between
Bites you talk of the fighters ours and theirs too
And of the boys who didn't get through of ships
Going down exploding in air the bullets that
Missed you by a hair your ship full of holes poor
Joe's dead he caught a flak fragment right
Through the head then head for your sack
About 9:00 or 10:00 a letter from home another from
Ben "I love you so" she wrote then you know
You've won for a gunners day
Is never done

LADY Scott AND CREW

In a prisoner of war camp just after the fight
I had nothing to do so decided to write
To write of my crew and tell you of their fate
And the training we had while back in the states
Now ours was no exception just an ordinary crew
We were picked at random like they always do
Just ordinary lads who were eager to fly
To give their all even if it meant to die

We were not flag wavers but were ready to give
Our last ounce of blood that others might live
By others I mean our daughters and sons
And of their fate if faced by the Guns — Huns
We first met at avon
Of getting acquainted and learning their ways
So important a factor for a crew to work
In harmony with one another not to shirk

Training was hard we were just like a team
Preparing for action you know what I mean
Bomb runs were made and fighters were met
We all fought like demons I'll never forget
Fighting positions were maned by a crew
Training for a job we knew what to do
The interphone system so important to all
Fighters at nine o'clock here comes the call

135

Tracking the target so vital a factor
Smooth operation was what we were after
A few short burst in a vital place
Would stop the fighters and end the chase
Mock battles were fought day after day
Training for combat "the Uncle Sam way"
Then came the day our folks became frantic
Twas time for take off across the atlantic

A new fort was ready we were bursting with pride
Eager to start on that long fateful ride
Picked out for combat and ready for strife
Lady Scott was named the pilots wife
A cold front was met while on our trip
Ice on our wings while in mother natures grip
Thanks to our wing boots we made it just fine
We all thought of ditching in that sally brine

We landed in England with no gas to spare
No one to greet us just parkit there
A lot of difference than when lindberg flew
Greeted by millions for making it through
More gunnery training we thought all bosh
Starting school again upat the wash
Studying our turrets and manning our guns
preparing for combat with the guns

136

Assigned to a sqd. a very old group
Flying in weather that resembled soup
"Jack the ripper" and the "Memphis Bell"
Finished their tour in that awful hell
I'll never forget that first bombing run
Wading through flak sent up by the
Riding my turret and saying a prayer
Thinking of loved ones safe over there

Limping back home with damage galore
Riding the deck over the English shore
Nevers still shakey after reaching our base
Mission completed end of the chase
Day after day we continued to fly
Missions were mounting as time flew by
Could it be possible to finish our tour?
Loved ones were praying we knew for sure

Some two hundred hrs of combat flying
We went through hell there is no denying
Mission after mission we gave our best
God we were tired and needed a rest
That fatal day we were shot from the sky
Twas destiny that said some must die
Two engines on fire and limping in flame
A target for fighters and their murderous aim

137

Captured and thrown in a prison cell
All thoughts of others it was hell
Long days in solitary with little to eat
Dreaming of loved ones a wife so sweet
Somewhere on an airtrip up in the sky
Pilot and crew members all waiting to fly
Con-trails can always be seen
No fighters no flak all is serene

Fond memories i'll cherish to my dying days
Of two brave men that were taken away
The things you fought for will live forever
A lasting peace only God can sever.

11-14-44

Dec 24th 44.
French SAButores
P.O.W.'s

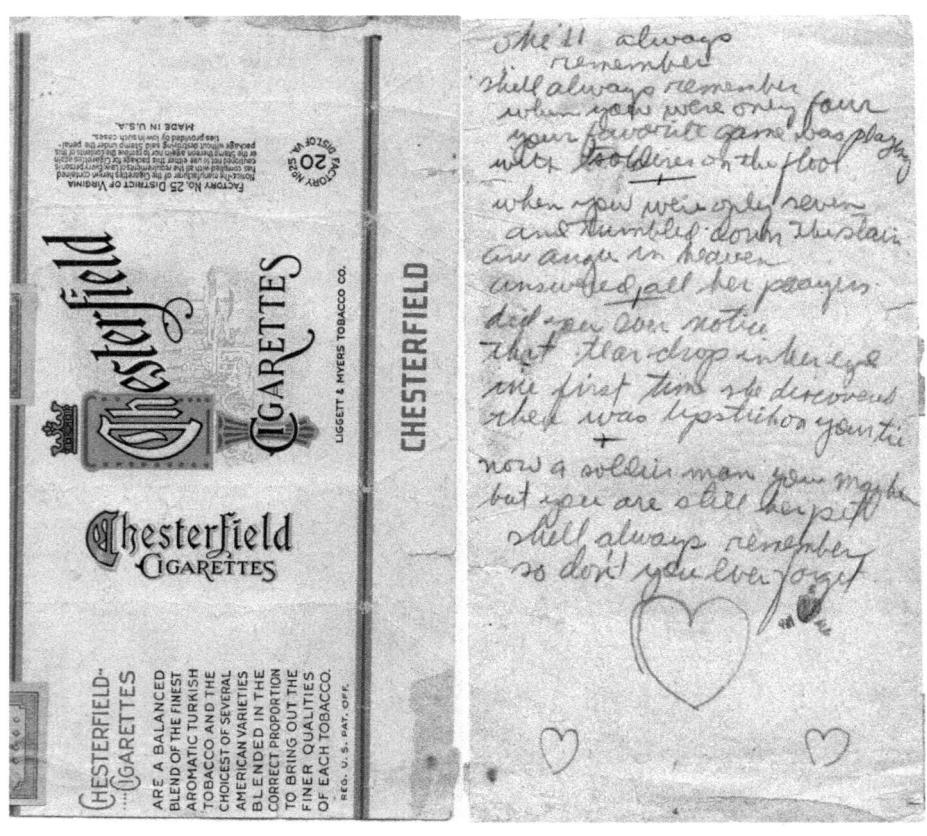

Appendix B: Copy of Letter

July 9, 1945

Dear Mr. & Mrs. Maltbie,

I hope this will find you all well and happy. We are all well here and that goes for my daughter too one you haven't met yet but I hope you do soon. Mrs. Maltbie I don't know how to begin about Lloyd. Nell told me you wanted to know about it all and that is why I am writing. I wouldn't want to write and hurt you any more than you have already been hurt for nothing on earth. I guess if it had been me instead of Lloyd Mom and Nell would want to know too. About all I know and can tell is that I don't think Lloyd felt any pain. We were hit in the bomb bay of the plane and Lloyd was very near the bomb bay and could have been hit causing him not to get out.

It all happened so quick that we didn't have much time for anything except to get out. The co-pilot said he didn't look back to see Lloyd. I cannot put into words how sorry I am that such a good boy like Maltbie had to go in this war. I am sure that if any boy ever goes to Heaven Lloyd will. He was the best boy I have ever known and I am not writing this to make you happy because I know you know how Lloyd was and I know the Army didn't change Lloyd any because he was good all the time I knew him. He liked his job and did his duty as he was
supposed to do.

He never missed a class while we were in training and could always be depended upon. Lt. Scott thought a lot of Lloyd Maltbie so did we all. Everyone that ever met him liked him and couldn't help it.

The Germans told me he was buried in a cemetery near Magdeburg. I don't now if his body was burned or not. The plane did go down on fire but exploded in the air Mrs. Maltbie I don't know if I should have wrote you that or not. Please forgive me if I did wrong. Jim and the rest said they was coming out to see you. I wish I could go with them but I have hurt my back and know I couldn't make the trip now. I do hope I can come out there soon. I might be stationed there someplace and if I do I will certainly come to see you all.

I thank you for the present you sent Bealer Gwen and if there is anything I can ever do for you please let me know because I will be glad to do anything for the parents of such a good boy and my friend. May God bless you always.
Love,
Bealer

Appendix C: Testimony of Dr. Caplan

For the War Crimes Office, Civil Affairs Division, WDSS
United States of America

Perpetuation of Testimony of Dr. Leslie Caplan (Formerly Major, MC, ASN 0-41343)
Taken at: Minnesota Military District, The Armory, 500 So. 6th St. Minneapolis, 15, Minn.
Date: 31 December 1947
In the Presence of: Lt. Col. William C. Hoffmann, AGD Executive Officer, Minnesota Military District, The Armory, 500 So. 6th St. Minneapolis, I5, Minn.

Questions:

Q. State your name, permanent home address, and occupation.
A. Leslie Caplan, Dr., 1728 Second Ave. So., Minneapolis, Minnesota; Resident Fellow in Psychiatry, University of Minnesota & Veterans Hospital, Minneapolis, Minn.

Q. State the date and place of your birth and of what country you are a citizen.
A. 8 March 1908, Steubenville, Ohio; citizen of the United States of America.

Q. State briefly your medical education and experience.
A. Ohio State University, B.A., 1933; MD 1936; University of Michigan Post Graduate work in Public Health; University of Minnesota Graduate School; one year general internship, Providence Hospital, Detroit, Michigan; 4 years general practice of medicine in Detroit, Michigan 1937-1941; 4 years Flight Surgeon, U.S. Army i941-1945.

Q. What is your marital status?
A. I am married.

Q. On what date did you return from overseas?
A. 29 June 1945.

Q. Were you a prisoner of war?
A. Yes.

Q. At what places were you held and state the approximate dates?
A. Dernisch, Jugo-Slavia 13 October 1944 to 20 October 1944: Zagreb, Jugo-Slavia 27 October 1944 to 1 November 1944; Dulag Luft, Frankfort, Germany, 15 November 1944 to 22 November 1944; Stalag Luft #4 28 November 1944 to 6 February 1945; on forced march under jurisdiction of Stalag Luft #4 February 1945 to 30 March 1945; Fallingbostel Stalag II B March 30 1945 to April 6 1945; on forced march from 6 April 1945 to 2 May 1945.

Q. What unit were you with when captured?
A. 15th Air Force, 449 Bomb Group, 719th Squadron. I was Flight Surgeon for the 719th Squadron

Q. State what you know concerning the mistreatment of American prisoners of war at Stalag Luft #4.
A. The camp was opened about April 1944 and was an Air Force Camp. It was located at Gross Tychow about two miles from the Kiefheide railroad station. In the summer of 1944 the Russian offensive threatened Stalag Luft #6, 50 approximately 1000 Americans were placed on a ship for evacuation to Stalag Luft #4. Upon arrival at the railroad station, certain groups were forced to run the two miles to Stalag Luft #4 at the points of bayonets. Those who dropped behind were either bayoneted or were bitten on the legs by police dogs.

Q. Were these wounds serious enough to cause any deaths?
A. All were flesh wounds and no deaths were caused by the bayoneting.

Q. Did you see these men at the time of the bayoneting?
A. No. This happened prior to my arrival at Luft #4.

Q. Did you see any of the men who were bitten by dogs?
A. Yes, I personally saw the healed wounds on the legs of a fellow named Smith or Jones (I am not certain as to the name) who had been severely bitten. There were approximately fifty bites on each leg. It looked as though his legs had been hit with small buck shot. This man remained an invalid confined to his bed all the time I was at Luft #4.

Q. Do you know how many men were injured as a result of the bayonet runs?
A. I was told that about twenty men had been hospitalized as a result. Many other bayoneted men were not hospitalized due to limited medical facilities.

The Unseen Hand

Q. Who told you of these incidents?
A. Captain Wilbur E. McKee, 1462 So. Seventh St., Louisville, Ky., who was Chief Camp Doctor. He should have some authentic records. Captain Henry E. Wysen, 346 E. Havenswood Ave., Youngstown, Ohio, also knew of the incidents. There were also two enlisted men who were elected by the soldiers as Camp leaders and known officially as "American Man of Confidence" who could give an account of the camp and of the bayoneting. The chief "American Man of Confidence" was camp leader and should have complete records of the incident. His name is Frank Paules, 101 Regent St., Wilkes-Barre, Pennsylvania.

Francis A. Troy, Box 233, Edgerton, Wyoming, the other enlisted man, and "American Man of Confidence" should also verify the incidents. Both of these enlisted men were also on the forced march when Stalag Luft #4 was evacuated.

Q. Do you know if the Commandant was responsible for the bayoneting and dog bites?
A. I did not know the Commandant and I do not know who was responsible. Captain Pickhardt, the officer in charge of the guards, is said to have incited the guards by telling them that American Airmen were gangsters who received a bonus for bombing German children and women. Most of the guards were older men and fairly reasonable, but other guards were pretty rough. "Big Stoop" was the most hated of the guards.

Q. For what reason was "Big Stoop" disliked?
A. He beat up on many of our men. He would cuff the men on the ears with an open hand sideway movement. This would cause pressure on the eardrums which sometimes punctured them.

Q. Could you give any specific incidents of such mistreatment by "Big Stoop"?
A. Yes. I treated some of the men whose eardrums had been ruptured by the cuffings administered by "Big Stoop".

Q. Can you describe "Big Stoop"?
A. He was about six feet, six inches tall, weight about 180 or 190 pounds, and was approximately fifty years old. His most outstanding characteristic was his large hands, which seemed out of proportion to those of a normal person.

Q. When you arrived at Stalag #4, were you subjected to the bayonet runs?
A. No. We were marched from the station to Luft #4, but not on the run. Some of the men were tired and we complained to "Big Stoop". He snarled at us, but personally went forward and slowed the column down.

Q. Did you have any duties assigned to you while a prisoner?
A. I was known as an Allied Medical Officer at Stalag #4 Camp Hospital and in charge of Section C while on the march.

Q. State what you know concerning the forced march from Stalag Luft #4?
A. In February 1945 the Russian Offensive threatened to engulf State Luft #4. On 6 February 1945 about 6,000 prisoners were ordered to leave the camp on foot after only a few hours notice. We left in three separate sections: A, C, and D. I marched with Section C which had approximately 2500 men. It was a march of great hardship. For 53 days we marched long distance in bitter weather and on starvation rations. We lived in filth and slept in open fields or barns. Clothing, medical facilities and sanitary facilities were utterly inadequate. Hundreds of men suffered from malnutrition, exposure, trench foot, exhaustion, dysentery, tuberculosis, and other diseases. No doubt many men are still suffering today as a result of that ordeal.

Q. Who was in charge of this march?
A. The commandant of Stalag Luft #4 was in charge of the three sections. Hauptman (Captain) Weinert was in charge of Section C that I marched with. All the elements of Stalag Luft #4 occupied a good bit of territory and there was frequent overlapping of the various sections.

Q. How much distance was covered in this march?
A. While under the jurisdiction of Stalag Luft #4, we covered an estimated 555 kilometers (330 miles). I kept a record, which I still have of distances covered, rations issued, sick men abandoned, and other pertinent data. This record is far from complete especially about records of the sick, but the record of rations and distances covered is complete.

Q. How much food was issued to the men on this march?
A. According to my records, during the 53 days of the march, the Germans issued us rations which I have since figured out contained a

total of 770 calories per day. The German ration was mostly in potatoes and contained very little protein, far from enough to maintain strength and health. However, in addition we were issued Red Cross food which for the same 53 day period averaged 566 calories per day. This means that our caloric intake per day on the march amounted to 1336 calories. This is far less than the minimum required to maintain body weight, even without the physical strenuous activity we compelled to undergo in the long marches.

The area we marched through was rural and there were no food shortages there. We all felt that the German officers in our column could have obtained more supplies for us. They contended that the food we saw was needed elsewhere. They further contended that the reason we received so little Red Cross supplies was that the Allied Air Force (of which we were "Gangster members) had disrupted the German transportation that carried Red Cross supplies. This argument was disproved later when we continued our march under the jurisdiction of another prison camp; namely Stalag #IIB. This was during the last month of the war when German transportation was at its worst. Even so, we received a good ration of potatoes almost daily and received frequent issues of Red Cross, far more than we were given under the jurisdiction of Stalag Luft #4.

Q. What sort of shelter was provided during the 53 day march?
A. Mostly we slept in barns. We were usually herded into these barns so closely that it was impossible for all men to find room to lie down. It was not unusual for many men to stand all night or to be compelled to sleep outside because there was no room inside. Usually there was some straw for some of us to lie on but many had to lie in barn filth or in dampness. Very frequently there were large parts of the barn (usually drier and with more straw) that were denied to us. There seemed to be no good reason why we should have to sleep in barnyard filth or stand in a crowded barn while other sections of the barn were not used. The Germans sometimes gave no reason for this but at other times, it was made clear to us that if we slept in the clean straw its value to the animals would be less because we would make it dirty. At other times barns were denied to us because the Germans stated having PWs in the barn might cause a fire that would endanger the livestock. It was very obvious that the welfare of German cattle was placed above our welfare. On 14 February 1945 Section C

of Stalag Luft #4 had marched approximately 35 kilometers. There were many stragglers and sick men who could barely keep up. That night the entire column slept in a cleared area in the woods near Schweinemunde. It had rained a good bit of the day and the ground was soggy, but it froze before morning. We slept on what was littered by the feces of dysenteric prisoners who had stayed there previously. There were many barns in the vicinity, but no effort was made to accommodate us there. There were hundreds of sick men in the column that night. I slept with one that was suffering from pneumonia.

Q. What were the conditions on this march as regards drinking water?
A. Very poor. Our sources of water were unsanitary surface water and well water often of questionable sanitary quality. At times so little water was issued to us that men drank whatever they could. While there was snow on the ground, it was common for the men to eat snow whether it was dirty or not. At other times some men drank from ditches that others had used as latrines. I personally protested this condition many times. The German doctor from Stalag Luft #4 (Capt. Sommers or Sonners) agreed that the lack of sanitary water was the principal factor responsible for the dysentery that plagued our men. It would have been a simple matter to issue large amounts of boiled water which would have been safe regardless of its source. At times we were issued adequate amounts of boiled water but at other times, not enough safe water was available. We often appealed to be allowed to collect firewood and boil water ourselves in the many boilers that were standard equipment on almost every German farm. This appeal was granted irregularly. When it was granted the men lined up in the cold for hours to await the tedious distribution. Another factor that forced an unnecessary hardship on us was the fact that when we first left Stalag Luft #4, the men were not permitted to take along a drinking utensil. The first few issues of boiled water were therefore not widely distributed for there were no containers for the men to collect the water in. As time went on, each man collected a tin can from the Red Cross food supplies and this filthy container was the sole means of collecting water or the soup that was sometimes issued to us.

Q. What medical facilities were available on the march from Stalag Luft #4?
A. They were pitiful. From the very start large numbers of men began to

fall behind. Blisters became infected and many men collapsed from hunger, fear, malnutrition, exhaustion, or disease. We organized groups of men to aid the hundreds of stragglers. It was common for men to drag themselves along in spite of intense suffering. Many men marched along with large abscesses on their feet or frostbite of extremities. Many others marched with temperatures as high as 105 degrees Fahrenheit. I personally slept with men suffering from Erysipelas, Diphtheria, Pneumonia, Malaria, Dysentery and other diseases. The most common disease was dysentery for this was an inevitable consequence of the filth we lived in and the unsanitary water we drank. This was so common and so severe, that all ordinary rules of decency were meaningless. Hundreds of men on this march suffered so severely from dysentery that they lost control of their bowel movements because of severe cramps and soiled themselves. Wherever our column went, there was a trail of bloody movements and discarded underwear (which was sorely needed for warmth). At times the Germans gave us a few small farm wagons to carry our sick. The most these wagons ever accommodated was 35 men but we had hundreds of men on the verge of collapse. It was our practice to load the wagon. As a man would collapse he would be put on the wagon and some sick man on the wagon would be taken off the wagon to make way for his exhausted comrade. When our column would near a permanent PW camp we were never allowed to leave all of our sick. I do not know what happened to most of the sick men that were left at various places along the march.

Q. What medical supplies were issued to you by the Germans on the march from Stalag Luft #4?
A. Very few. When we left the camp we carried with us a small amount of medical supplies furnished us by the Red Cross. At times the Germans gave us pittance of drugs. They claimed they had none to spare. At various times, I asked for rations of salt. Salt is essential for the maintenance of body strength and of body fluids and minerals. This was particularly needed by our men because hundreds of them had lost tremendous amounts of body fluids and minerals as the result of dysentery. The only ration of salt that I have a record of or can recall was one small bag of salt weighing less than a pound. This was for about 2500 men. I feel there is no excuse for this inadequate ration of salt.

Q. To your knowledge, did any sick man die as a result of neglect by the Germans on the march from Stalag Luft #4?

A. Yes. The following named men died as a result of neglect. All of these men have been declared dead by the Casualty Branch of the Adjutant General's Office:

NAME
George W. Briggs S/Sgt.
John C. Clark S/Sgt.
Edward B. Coleman S/Sgt.
George F. Grover S/Sgt.
William Lloyd S/Sgt.
Harold H. Mack T/Sgt.
Robert M. Trapnell S/Sgt.

It is likely that there were other deaths that I do not know about.

Q. Did all these deaths occur while the men were directly under the control of Stalag Luft #4?

A. No. As I mentioned before, our sick men were left at various places and I never saw them again. Some of these men died after we were out of the jurisdiction of Stalag Luft 4.

Q. What were the circumstances which led to the deaths of these men?

A. At 0200 on 9 April 1945 at a barn in Wohlen, Germany, Sgt. George W. Briggs was suddenly overcome by violent shaking of the entire body and soon after he went into a coma. This patient was sent to a German hospital. We were then under the jurisdiction of POW Camp Stalag II B and they voluntarily sent this patient to a hospital. This is in marked contrast to the treatment received when we were under the jurisdiction of Stalag Luft 4 when every hospitalization was either refused or granted after a long series of waiting for guards, waiting for permission to see Capt. Weinert, and waiting his decision. In spite of the prompt hospitalization, this patient dies on 11 April 1945. No doubt this death was largely caused by being weakened on the first part of the march while under the jurisdiction of Stalag Luft 4. On 9 March 1945 while on the march in Germany, Capt. Sommers who was the German doctor for Stalag Luft 4, personally notified me that John C. Clark had died the previous night of pneumonia. He had not been hospitalized and had received very little medical care. I never saw this patient, but he was seen in a barn in the terminal stages of his illness by Capt. Pollack of the

Royal Medical Corps who told me about it later on. On 13 April 1945 while on the march in Germany, Edward B. Coleman collapsed from severe abdominal pain and weakness. I made a diagnosis of an acute abdominal emergency superimposed on a previously weakened condition which was the result of malnutrition and dysentery. He was hospitalized but according to the records of the Adjutant General, he died 15 April 1945. He had had both legs amputated because of gangrene secondary to frostbite. He told me that S/Sgt Vincent Soddaro ASN 32804649 of Brooklyn, New York had also had both legs amputated because of gangrene and frostbite. Sgt. Edwards and Sgt. Soddaro had been in the same German hospital.

Q. What other mistreatment did you suffer on the march from Stalag Luft 4?
A. There were beatings by the guards at times but it was a minor problem. At 1500 hours on 28 March 1945 a large number of our men were loaded on freight cars at Ebbsdorf, Gem We were forced in at the rate of 60 men or more to a car. This was so crowded that there was not enough room for all men to sit at the same time. We remained in these jammed boxcars until 0030 hours March 30, 1945 when our train left Ebbsdorf. During this 33 hour period few men were allowed out of the cars for the cars were sealed shut most of the time. The suffering this caused was unnecessary for there was a pump with a good supply of water in the railroad yards a short distance from the train. At one time I was allowed to fetch some water for a few of our men who were suffering from dysentery. Many men had dysentery at the time and the hardship of being confined to the freight cars was aggravated by the filth and stench resulting from men who had to urinate and defecate inside the cars. We did not get off these freight cars until we reached Fallingbostel around noon of 30 March 1945 and then we marched to Stalag 11B. The freight cars we were transported in had no marking on them to indicate that they were occupied by helpless prisoners of war. There was constant aerial activity in the area at the time and there was a good chance of being strafed.

Q. Was the suffering that resulted from the evacuation march from Stalag Luft 4 avoidable?
A. Certainly a large part of the suffering was avoidable. As I mentioned before, we marched through rural Germany and there was no lack of

food there. There were always many large barns available that could have been used by us. There was always firewood available that could have been used to boil water and thus give us a supply of safe drinking water. There were many horses and wagons available that could have been used to transport our sick mer There were many men in our column who were exhausted and who could have been left for a rest at prison camps that we passed on the march.

On 30 March 1945 we left the jurisdiction of Stalag Luft 4 when we arrived at Stalag Luft On 6 April 1945 we again went on a forced march under the jurisdiction of Stalag 11B. Our first march had been in a general westerly direction for the Germans were then running from the Russians. The second march was in a general easterly direction for the Germans were running from the American and British forces. Because of this, during the march under the jurisdiction of Stalag 11B we doubled back and covered a good bit of the same territory we just come over a month before. We doubled back for over 200 kilometers and it took 26 days before British forces liberated us. During those 26 days we were accorded much better treatment. We received a ration of potatoes daily besides other food including horse meat. We always barns to sleep in although the weather was much milder than when we had previously cover this same territory. During these 26 days we received about 1235 calories daily from the Germans and an additional 1500 calories daily from the Red Cross for a total caloric intake. I believe that if the officers of Stalag Luft 4 had made an effort they too could have secured us as much rations and shelter.

Q. To what officers from Stalag Luft 4 did you complain?
A. I only saw the commandant of Stalag Luft 4 once on the entire march and I was not allowed to talk to him then. Mostly I complained to Capt. Weinert who was in charge of "C" column that I was with most of the time.

Q. Can you describe Capt. Weinert?
A. He was a little taller than average and well built. He was in his forties but looked much younger until he took his cap off and exposed his bald head. He was an Air Corps officer and was said to have been a prisoner of the Allies in North Africa and later repatriated for a physical disability. I never saw any certain evidence of such a disability. He rarely marched but rode in his own wagon. Some of the men said he had an

arm injury but I never saw any definite evidence of this. Maybe this was because I only saw him on rather formal military occasions when he would stand or sit in a rigid manner almost as if he were at attention. I never saw him for long periods of time. He spoke excellent English but it was a favorite trick of his to act as if he did not understand English. Usually he spoke to me through an interpreter, but several times we spoke in English.

Q. Are there any other incidents that should be reported.
A. There is one other incident I would like to report. On 16 February 1945 we were on the road west of the Oder River in the general area of Schweinemunde. I was then marching with a party of several hundred of our stragglers who were tagging along behind our main column. We met a small group of other prisoners on the road. I was allowed to talk to these men briefly and obtained the following information: these men were from PW camp Stalag 2B, which had originally been at Hammerstein. They were all sick and had left their column to be taken to a hospital. On arrival at the hospital they were denied admission and continued the march with little or no rations. These men appeared to be on the verge of exhaustion. Two had obvious fevers with severe cough, which was probably pneumonia or tuberculosis. About 20 of these men were Americans. One had on a foreign uniform and I thought he was an Italian. There was a tall British sergeant with them. One of the men carried a small wooden chest with the name of "Joe McDaniels" or "Joe McWilliams" on it. He told me that he had been acting as Chaplain at Stalag 2B. Another man was a tall, slender fellow from Schenectady, New York. (After I was liberated I met an ex-prisoner from Stalag 2B who thought this fellow was J. Luckhurst of 864 Stanley, Schenectady, New York.) This fellow said he was suffering from recurrent malaria. These men were so weak they could scarcely stand. The German sergeant in charge of our small section at the time recognized their plight and got a Wehrmacht truck to take them to our next stop. We received no rations that night, but did get a small issue of hot water. The next day these men were placed on wagons and stayed with us. They again received no rations and again were sheltered in crowded barns. On 18 February 1945, I personally protested to Capt. Weinert about these men, although he had known about them previously. I pointed out that these men were exhausted and might soon die. I requested rations, rest, and hospitalization for them.

Capt. Weinert said they were not his responsibility, inasmuch as they were not originally from Stalag Luft 4. I objected to this and stated that these men were now in our column and that he was responsible for their lives and health. He then agreed to leave these men behind. The next day, Capt. Weinert told me these men had been transferred to another command. I never saw the men again, but I heard a rumor that one of them had died.

Q. Do you have anything further to add?
A. No.

(signed)
Leslie Caplan, M.D.
State of Minnesota
County of Hennepin
I, Dr. Leslie Caplan, of lawful age, being duly sworn on oath, state that I have read the foregoing transcription of my interrogation and all answers contained therein are true to the best of my knowledge and belief.
(signed)
Leslie Caplan, M.D.

Subscribed and sworn to before me, this 5 day of January 1948.

(signed)
William C. Hoffmann
Lt. Colonel, AGD
Summary Court

CERTIFICATE

I, William C. Hoffman, Lt. Col. Certify that Dr. Leslie Caplan personally appeared before me on December 31, 1947 and testified concerning war crimes; and that the foregoing is an accurate transcription of the answers given by him to the several questions set forth.

The Unseen Hand

About the Author

Bealer W. Moore (1922-2002) was born in Prince George County, VA, in 1922. He married Clara Garnell Moore in 1942. In 1943, he enlisted in the Army Air Corps. As a Technical Sergeant, he served as a Radio Operator on a B-17 until he was shot down over Germany. He was a POW for the remainder of the war.

Bealer received the following medals recognizing his service in the US Military:

2 Air Medals (one for helping the French Resistance)
The Prisoner of War Medal
The Purple Heart

In civilian life, he worked for the US Postal Service until 1976. After retirement, Bealer and Nell moved to Belews Creek, NC, where he enjoyed painting, gardening, and playing guitar/banjo until he passed in 2002.

www.ingramcontent.com/pod-product-compliance
Lightning Source LLC
Chambersburg PA
CBHW060151050426
42446CB00013B/2773